EXPLORE THE WORLD

GW00732827

GRAN CANARIA

Authors:
Bernd F. Gruschwitz,
Michael Reimer,
Wolfgang Taschner

An Up-to-date travel guide
with 55 color photos
and 4 maps

NELLES

LEGEND / IMPRINT

Dear Reader: Being up-to-date is the main goal of the Nelles series. Our correspondents help keep us abreast of the latest developments in the travel scene, while our cartographers see to it that maps are also kept completely current. However, as the travel world is constantly changing, we cannot guarantee that all the information contained in our books is always valid. Should you come across a discrepancy, please contact us at: Nelles Verlag, Schleissheimer Str. 371 b, 80935 Munich, Germany, tel. (089) 3571940, fax. (089) 35719430, e-mail: Nelles.Verlag@t-online.de

Note: Distances and measurements, including temperatures, used in this guide are metric. For conversion information, please see the *Guidelines* section of this book.

LEGEND

★★ ★★	Main Attraction (on map) (in text)	Santa Cruz *(Town)* Iglesia *(Sight)* Places Highlighted in Yellow Appear in Text	Expressway
★ ★	Worth Seeing (on map) (in text)	International/National Airport	Principal Highway
❽	Orientation Number in Text and on Map	Nature Reserve	Main Road
▪	Public or Significant Building	Teide (3717) Mountain (altitude in meters)	Provincial Road
▪	Hotel	\ 13 / Distance in Kilometers	Secondary Road
▪	Shopping Center	Beach	Pedestrian Zone
✝	Church	Ancient Site	Car Ferry
☀	View Point	Cave	$ $ $ Luxury Hotel Category
		Tourist Information	$ $ Moderate Hotel Catego $ Budget Hotel Category (for price information see "Accomodation" in Guidelines section)

GRAN CANARIA
© Nelles Verlag GmbH, 80935 Munich
   All rights reserved

First Edition 2000
ISBN 3-88618-282-7 (Nelles Travel Pack)
ISBN 3-88618-775-6 (Nelles Pocket)
Printed in Slovenia

Publisher:	Günter Nelles
Managing Editor:	Berthold Schwarz
Editor:	Chase Stewart
Translators:	David Ingram, Eva Döring

Picture Editor:	K. Bärmann-Thümmel
Cartography:	Nelles Verlag GmbH
Lithos:	Priegnitz, Munich
Printing:	Gorenjski Tisk

- S02 -

TABLE OF CONTENTS

LIST OF MAPS

OCÉANO

ISLAS

LA PALMA

Pico de
la Cruz
(2351)
Santa
Cruz

Los Llanos
de Aridane

TENERIFE

San Cristóbal
de la Laguna

Puerto de
la Cruz

SANTA C

Pico del Teide
(3715)

LA GOMERA

(1487)
San
Sebastián

Los Cristianos

Granadilla
de Abona

EL HIERRO

Valverde

Malpaso
(1501)

OCÉANO

CANARY ISLANDS

0   50 km

ATLÁNTICO

ALEGRANZA

MONTAÑA CLARA

GRACIOSA

LANZAROTE

CANARIAS
(SPAIN)

(608)

Arrecife

Playa Blanca

Corralejo

LOS LOBOS

FUERTEVENTURA

Puerto del
Rosario

Betancuria
(724)

Gáldar

LAS PALMAS

Pico de las
Nieves
(1949)

GRAN CANARIA

Jandía
(807)

Gran Tarajal

Moro del Jable

Maspalomas

Laayoune

ATLÁNTICO

MAROC

Lemsid

7

Prehistory

16 million years ago Gran Canaria emerges after heavy volcanic eruptions on the seabed of the Atlantic Ocean as the third Canary Island, after Lanzarote and Fuerteventura.

Circa 1100 B.C. Phoenicians, and later the Carthaginians, head for the Canary Islands. A period of historical oblivion follows after the Romans destroy Carthage in 146 B.C.

Circa 400 B.C. The first natives settle the islands. There is much evidence today that they originated from Berber tribes from the North African coast. There is still speculation today, however, on how they managed to get over.

Pre-Hispanic Times

Circa A.D. 1 The Romanized Berber king Juba II of Mauretania tries to conquer the Canary Islands with his fleet. The expedition, however, fails.

A.D. 100-160 Claudius Ptolemy draws the zero meridian through the Canary Island of El Hierro, which is considered the known world's westernmost point right up until the discovery of America.

Up to the Middle Ages The aboriginal population of the Canary Islands carries on living in their early Stone-Age culture, undisturbed by any foreign influence. There is hardly any contact between the various islands of the archipelago. Although wars and epidemics claim heavy casualties in mainland Europe, the natives live a peaceful life in complete harmony with nature.

The Conquista

1330-1342 The Portuguese, Spaniards and Mallorcans invade the Canary Islands in search of slaves.

1344 Luis de la Cerda is appointed king of the Canary Islands by Pope Clement, however, he never sets foot on the archipelago.

1402 The Norman nobleman Jean de Béthencourt conquers Lanzarote.

1405 Fuerteventura and La Gomera also submit to Jean de Béthencourt. Maciot de Béthencourt is appointed viceroy of the islands. Jean de Béthencourt's attempts to conquer Gran Canaria fail.

1418 Count de Nibla buys the Canary Islands from Maciot de Béthencourt.

1478 Founding of Las Palmas after the landing of captain Juán Rejón on Gran Canaria. First attacks on the Guanches, the aboriginal inhabitants, who withdraw into the mountains.

1479 In the treaties of Alcácovas and Toledo, the Canary Islands are ceded to Spain.

1483 The aboriginal population of Gran Canaria surrenders to the Spaniards and accepts forced baptism as a sign of subjugation.

1492 Christopher Columbus starts his voyage of discovery from the Canary Islands. He is believed to have had repairs carried out on his ships on the island of Gran Canaria.

Lava streams that solidified while flowing attest to the volcanic origin of the island.

1496 Tenerife comes under foreign rule as the last island of the Canary archipelago.

Spanish Domination

1500-1554 The cultivation of sugar cane at first causes the local economy to flourish, but the product soon loses ground in the face of overseas competition and eventually disappears altogether. During this period, vast wooded areas fall victim to the introduction of sugar cane.

16th to 17th centuries The natives are forced to adapt to Spanish customs. The Canary Islands are repeatedly attacked by pirates from England, France, the Netherlands and Portugal. Particularly bad memories remain of Sir Francis Drake's assault in 1595 and of a devastating raid by Dutch pirates in 1599.

17th to 20th centuries There are several waves of emigration among the inhabitants of Gran Canaria to Central and South America due to economic necessity.

Island impressions for every taste – they have drawn tourists here for more than a century.

1730-1736 Heavy volcanic eruptions make vast areas of Lanzarote uninhabitable.

1797 The last of numerous attempts to conquer the islands; it is Lord Nelson's only defeat.

1820 Las Palmas becomes the capital of Gran Canaria.

1821 Santa Cruz de Tenerife becomes the administrative capital of all of the Canary Islands.

1830-70 The production and exportation of red dye from cochineal insects enables economic recovery.

From 1850 Cultivation of dwarf bananas. The old plantations still adorn many valleys.

1852 Queen Isabella II declares the impoverished islands a free-trade zone. The shipyard industry and trade flourish.

1855 Completion of the harbor of Las Palmas under the engineer León y Castillo.

1880-1890 A number of hotels are built on Gran Canaria by British investors. The first tourists come to the island.

Circa 1900 Las Palmas develops into a significant supply harbor for transatlantic steamships.

The 20th Century

1912 Gran Canaria receives a self-administrating body, the island council (*calbido insular*).

1927 Las Palmas de Gran Canaria becomes the capital of the western part of the archipelago (Gran Canaria, Fuerteventura and Lanzarote). Santa Cruz de Tenerife becomes the seat of government for Tenerife, La Gomera, La Palma and El Hierro.

1936 General Franco begins the Spanish Civil War from the Canary Islands. His victory leads to a dictatorship in Spain lasting from 1939 until the Generalissimo's death in 1975.

1956 Landing of the very first tourist charter flight on Gran Canaria. A flight from Düsseldorf takes over eight hours at the time.

1971 Last volcanic eruption on Gran Canaria.

1975 After Franco's death, King Juan Carlos becomes the head of state.

1976 Members of several political groups and trade unions of the Canary Islands issue a document demanding that all rights and political liberties for the various nationalities and regions within Spain be allowed.

1977 For the first time there are more than one million tourists a year on Gran Canaria.

1978 First democratic elections in Spain

1982 The Canary Islands are assigned the status of an autonomous province of Spain and are allowed to vote for their first parliament.

1986 Spain joins the European Community. The Canary Islands are granted special status.

1990 A university is founded in Las Palmas.

1999 The Canary Islands are guaranteed the highest level of European Union grants for a further six years.

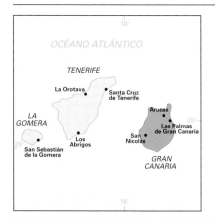

GRAN CANARIA
Holiday Island to Suit Every Taste

BEACHES IN THE SOUTH
THE IMPENETRABLE WEST
THE MILD NORTH
LAS PALMAS DE GRAN CANARIA
THE ARID EAST
THE INTERIOR

Broad Beaches, Craggy Coastline

After Tenerife, Gran Canaria is the biggest tourist attraction of the Canary Islands. Germans are top of the tourist list, making up almost a third of the visitors, followed by the British and Spaniards from the mainland. Most of the vacationers stay in the large hotel and apartment regions on the south coast of the island. Lonely beaches are few and far between around here, but if you appreciate a beach holiday with a mixture of relaxation and variety, visit the attractive sand beaches and the magnificent dune landscape of Maspalomas, and then indulge in all the water sports facilities before plunging into the nightlife.

The island's capital, Las Palmas, is also growing increasingly popular. It has good hotels and boarding houses, the beach of Las Canteras, elegant stores and a broad range of cultural activities. A new kind of tourism is also developing to cater for travelers with individual tastes: you can live in the renovated fincas, for instance, that are strewn all over the island. The

Previous pages: Parasailing over the Playa del Inglés. Maspalomas – the "little Sahara" of the south. An important branch of the local economy – tomatoes. Left: Calle Mayor de Triana – stylish shopping street (Las Palmas).

green north of the island is also very popular now: bike tours and hiking trips can be taken through places like the pine forest of Tamadaba. Traditional buildings with carved wooden balconies and richly decorated churches can still be found in towns such as Gáldar, Teror and Telde.

Gran Canaria's beauty is mainly evident in the central mountain region, with the 1,949-meter-high Pico de las Nieves and the 1,817-meter-high Roque Nublo. Cragged rock formations at the summits, resembling prehistoric steles, were considered holy by the islands' ancient inhabitants; to today's visitors they are more reminiscent of Wild West movies. Deep gorges *(barrancos)* and glittering reservoirs add to the attraction of this breathtaking mountain scenery.

Arrival

If you're traveling to Gran Canaria by ferry, you usually arrive in Las Palmas harbor; the ferry from Tenerife also travels to Puerto de las Nieves, the harbor of Agaete. Most international visitors arrive at the only major airport, the **Aeropuerto de Gando** in the east of the island. Located 22 kilometers from the capital, the airport is a hub of international, national and interinsular air traffic, and provides all modern amenities, from banking services to rental cars. A well-paved highway connects the Aeropuerto de Gando with the capital and the tourist centers to the south. Buses leave for Las Palmas every 20 minutes, and there are numerous taxis available, too.

BEACHES IN THE SOUTH

Most vacationers take their package holidays in the hotels that line the sun-soaked south of Gran Canaria. It's not surprising, therefore, that the apartment complexes along the beaches here are usually booked out in high season.

You can lie in the sand and relax, take part in the extensive hotel activity programs, or try your hand at sports: windsurfing, diving, water-skiing, paragliding, horseback riding and golf are just as much on offer as tennis, squash, mountain biking and volleyball. There's also a lively multinational pub scene.

Once you've grown accustomed to the uniform-looking phony urbanity of it all, you'll soon realize that life in the hotel complexes is comfortable, and that the attractive, subtropical parks and gardens are often a colorful way of concealing an odd architectural eyesore. Naturally, there are some regions that stand out positively from the rest, one of them being Puerto de Mogán (see p. 21) on the southwest coast, where planners were careful to harmonize the new buildings with the old town center and the surrounding landscape. This kind of success, however, is rare, and the homogeneity of Manrique's Lanzarote is conspicuous by its absence. He did give local architects pause for thought, however, and even though financial considerations still tend to outweigh esthetic ones, there seems to be a gradual realization among planners that landscape must play a part.

Highway GC1 from the airport to the south runs along a broad and almost desert-like strip of coast, nearly parallel to the road. Barren, rocky mountains can

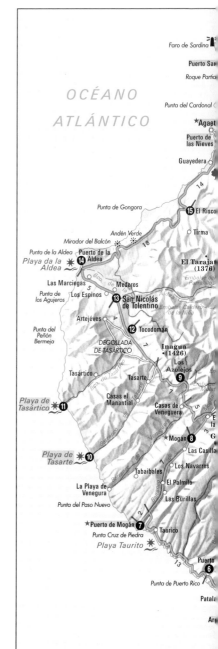

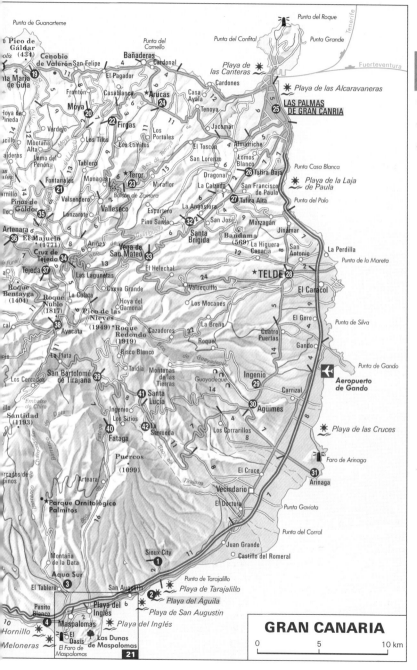

GRAN CANARIA

17

be seen along the horizon to the west. Shortly before the **Playa de Tarajalillo** you can change from the highway to the main road. The airplane beside it indicates the presence of the **Aeroclub de Gran Canaria** flying club.

Branch off to the right through the **Cañon del Águila** to the western town of **Sioux City ❶**, where visitors tired of beaches can enjoy Wild West shows (buses run from Playa del Inglés and Maspalomas; closed Mondays).

The **Playa del Águila ❷** marks the start of a series of beaches connected to each other by promenades, and extending a distance of around eight kilometers as far as Playa del Inglés and the dunes of Maspalomas.

The father of surfing champion Björn Dunkerbeck has set up a surfing school on the Playa del Águila. The small, sandy beach with its clear water mainly attracts

Above: Playa de San Agustín – sun, sand and hordes of people. Right: Maspalomas – just perfect for surfing in a steady breeze.

young people. This whole stretch of coast, with its steady winds, is ideal for windsurfing. Even if you're a beginner, just go and ask for a lesson – you'll wobble around and get wet for the first hour or so, but it's astonishing how quickly you learn. Don't forget to wear sun protection, though – things can get very hot once you've learned how not to fall in all the time!

Next door, on the very neat and tidy **Playa de San Agustín**, all generations join together to relax in the sun. This part of the coast is especially popular with Germans. The beach extends for about two kilometers, and there are numerous apartment blocks and hotels with leafy parks around them. Guests can either swim in the sea or in the hotels' own pools. Pedestrian footbridges provide access to the beach from the hotels on the other side of the main road. As far as nightlife is concerned, the discos and bars of the hotels provide evening entertainment, and there's a casino in the luxurious *Melia Tamarindos Sol* beach hotel.

Playa del Ingles and Maspalomas – The Tourist Machine

If the beaches mentioned so far were reasonably quiet and peaceful, the **Playa del Inglés** ❶ is busy and loud. Either you love it or you hate it – some people come here only to leave in disgust, others spend years returning to the same place and can't seem to get enough of it. No worries about having to do without your local newspaper from back home, or not being able to speak Spanish: the waiters and shopkeepers are real linguistic geniuses. A seemingly endless stream of visitors moves along the beach in both directions all day long. You can watch windsurfers fighting the wind and waves, and yachts doing risky maneuvers.

Of course, this vacation location has a very busy nightlife, with bars, discos and amusement arcades. You can play bingo, eat Black Forest cake, drink Guinness and yodel with Bavarians. The massive shopping centers – especially the **Kasbah** ❷ on the Plaza del Teide and the **Yumbo**

❸ on Avenida de España – are packed full of jewelry, fashions, electronic articles, souvenirs and groceries from all over the world. It's strange that the built-up conglomeration of restaurants, souvenir shops and amusement arcades should be so close to an astonishingly beautiful and relatively unspoiled area: the Playa del Inglés is almost seamlessly connected with the magnificent, kilometer-wide dune area known as ****Las Dunas de Maspalomas** ❹. This is where all those masses of tourists get lost, and in the middle of the golden yellow sand dunes the (often nude) sunbathers are greeted by relaxing silence. Wandering through this protected natural park is like being in a miniature Sahara Desert – especially when a "camel caravan" moves by.

The area on the western edge of Maspalomas is called **El Oasis**. **La Charca** ❺, the remains of a lagoon with reeds around the edge, borders a grove of palm trees. Entering the lagoon area is forbidden, because the reeds are home to nesting waterfowl. The tallest lighthouse in all the Canary Islands, **El Faro de Maspalomas** ❻ (65 meters), marks the southernmost point of the island. Hotels, restaurants and stores have spread out beneath it. To the north of the lagoon is the starting point for the camel safaris, as well as the gold course and the squash courts. The **Holiday World** ❼ amusement park and the **Océano Parque Acuatico Maspalomas** ❽ water park are both ideal for families with children.

To the north of Maspalomas, in the suburb of El Tablero, you'll find the water park of **Aqua Sur** ❸ (on the right after you've passed under the highway), and an excursion high up into the rocky Barranco de Chamoriscan leads 12 kilometers later to the ***Parque Ornitológico Palmitos** (served regularly by bus from Playa del Ingles). This 200,000-square-meter area is an artificial biotope with around 1,000 palm trees, a cactus garden, an orchid and butterfly house, a seawater aquarium and 230 exotic species of bird, some of which have been allowed to fly freely. There's an amusing parrot show for the kids which should not be missed – the birds are trained to do all sorts of amazing feats, such as pedaling on unicycles, lying in deck chairs and actually doing some relatively simple math – and of course there's a souvenir shop and a snack bar here, too.

Six kilometers to the north of the Playa del Inglés (follow the signs to Fataga; there's also a bus connection), up on a hill, there's the "archeological show-park" of **Mundo Aborigen**, introducing visitors to the way the ancient inhabitants of the Canary Islands used to live, in an area covering 100,000 square meters. This place is definitely worth a visit. A village has been reconstructed, as have typical scenes from Canarian aboriginal life, along with their pets, plants and crafts. The whole thing is explained in several different languages, and there's also a live show in which the praises of the brave warriors are sung in their battle

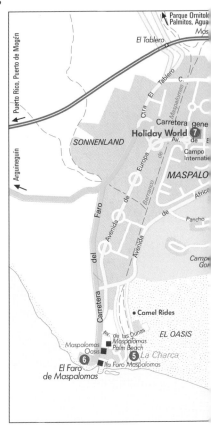

against the Spanish intruders. The usual snack and souvenir stands can also be found here.

Back at the coast you can either take the highway or the well-paved asphalt road, the 812, westwards. Near **Pasito Blanco** ❹ there is a yacht harbor and sailing school, as well as a private campsite. The quieter beaches between Maspalomas and Arguineguín are the **Playa de las Meloneras** and the **Playa del Hornillo**. The highway ends shortly before Arguineguín, and traffic now has to pass along the narrower coast road.

The one-time fishing village of **Arguineguín** ❺ does contain the usual hotel blocks, but its original center has remained largely intact – the only eyesore

Gran Canaria

PLAYA DEL INGLÉS /
MASPALOMAS

0   500   1000 m

to speak of being the nearby cement works. At the harbor there is a great restaurant, the *Cofradia de Pescadores*, which serves delicious seafood. A boat makes the Arguineguín – Puerto Rico – Puerto de Mogán trip several times a day (travel time about 90 minutes).

After Arguineguín it's one bay after another. The buildings at **Puerto Rico ❻** are particularly striking: the apartment complexes here have been packed together quite tightly on the mountain slopes, and it's astonishing how rigorously the tourist industry has exhausted the possibilities of this piece of real estate. The monotony is alleviated somewhat by the luxuriant greenery, which has successfully concealed a great deal of ar-

chitectural evil all over the island. Puerto Rico also has a yachting harbor and a broad sand beach, both of which provide numerous opportunities for different water sports, including windsurfing, sailing and waterskiing.

*Puerto de Mogán

Shortly before Puerto de Mogán, you can reach the grayish-black **Playa Taurito** by going through a barranco with small plantations. This beach, a favorite with backpackers and easy-going sunworshipers, is gradually being developed, but still has a pleasant relaxed atmosphere. Attempts have been made to create a kind of alternative holiday location

at the end of the Barranco de Mogán, the **Puerto de Mogán ❼**. Apart from a tower-like structure at the harbor exit, all the buildings have been kept purposely low, and are connected via promenades and little bridges. The colorful doors and window frames of the holiday apartments blend in very nicely with the gardens and parks. The harmony of the architecture is pleasantly refreshing after the numerous eyesores elsewhere.

One section, closed to cars, has been flooded with seawater to create what is locally referred to as "Little Venice." The pubs, bars and cafés are generally owned by non-residents. The local fishermen live slightly outside the village, up on a slope. The harbor, protected by a mighty quay wall, contains an armada of luxury yachts. The 300-meter-long, gently sloping sand beach of **Playa de Mogán** is actually artificial, even though it looks extremely realistic.

Above: Puerto de Mogán – a Canarian "Little Venice." Right: Not the smallest of tuna!

THE IMPENETRABLE WEST
Craggy Mountains, Remote Beaches

The west of Gran Canaria is one of its wildest but also most impressive regions. The road leads north from Puerto de Mogán through the Barranco de Mogán, and then heads up inland. This thinly-populated area contains banana, mango and papaya plantations. Before you reach the pretty town of Mogán, you'll see some oversized – sometimes man-sized – household utensils at the roadside, such as coffee pots, coffee mills and irons. They stand there almost all year long and are sometmes carried along on parades. There are also the remains of an old wind-mill; just the renovated shell. Foreign residents and artists have created their own individual refuge in the various elegant houses dotted around **★Mogán ❽**.

This town, idyllically situated on the slopes of the 932-meter-high **Guirre**, is a popular starting point for hikes and tours in jeeps through the surrounding area. One good excursion leads along a narrow track with hairpin bends, through the Barranco de Mogán, and to the reservoirs of **Embalse de Mulato**, **Embalse de Cueva de las Niñas** (with a cave), and **Embalse de Soria**. The track then continues inland as far as Ayacata (see p. 49). A word of warning, by the way: This stretch of road seems to be a permanent construction site, so beware of potholes and other obstacles.

The 810 bends dramatically westwards just past Mogán and then winds its way through some very rugged mountain scenery, with numerous barrancos all leading to the sea. The first one, the **Barranco de Veneguera**, has become a political issue because environmentalists want to protect it and its beach from tourists. The island government has, however, given the go-ahead for a project to build holiday apartments here, with accommodation for up to 20,000 people. At the present time it looks increasingly unlikely that the real estate developers can be stopped.

Carry on in the direction of San Nicolas de Tolentino, and beneath the 1,426-meter-high **Inagua** you'll reach a place known as **Los Azulejos** ❾, so named because of its resemblance to the blue tiles that often adorn Portuguese buildings. This is a fascinating geological formation: iron has colored several rock and pumice strata here bluish-green. There's a bar to quench your thirst, and information on a number of other hikes where you can see even more colorful rocks is also available here.

The next turnoff in the direction of the sea leads through the fertile Barranco de Tasarte as far as the black **Playa de Tasarte** ❿. Huts and fishing boats make the place extremely idyllic. The water is also quite shallow here, and is suitable for young bathers, too. Locals come here at weekends and the beach bar gets extremely crowded.

It's (still) a lot less busy at the neighboring **Playa de Tasártico** ⓫, which can

be reached via the Degollada de Tasártico Pass (550 meters) shortly before Tocodomán. The new road down in the valley will soon make the beach easily accessible. Getting into the water for a swim here is difficult because of the slippery rocks, though. At **Tocodomán** ⓬ there's a **Cactus Garden** with around two million specimens from all over the world.

San Nicolás de Tolentino

San Nicolás de Tolentino ⓭ is the main tomato-growing region on Gran Canaria. The fields, with their plastic sheets protecting the plants, can be seen from a long way off. Apart from the houses, the whole valley looks like something produced by Christo, the packaging artist.

San Nicolás is one of the oldest settlements on the island, and was the destination of numerous Christian missionaries from Mallorca during the 14th century. In a squabble over land rights which lasted for over 300 years, the villagers finally

managed to defeat the noble family of Villanueva del Prado in 1911 and obtain land for their own private cultivation.

From San Nicolás you can take a spectacular tour of the interior. A narrow asphalt road with plenty of bends (often with just one lane) leads through the canyon-like Barranco de la Aldea, one of the most impressive of its kind on the island. The route then continues through a craggy section of mountain landscape and past a chain of reservoirs before finally arriving at Artenara, at 1,250 meters the highest village on Gran Canaria.

If you prefer to stay on the coast, visit the pebble beach of **Playa de la Aldea**, located south of the fishing village of **Puerto de la Aldea ⓮**. Small restaurants serve delicious seafood, and the view of the sun setting behind the silhouette of Tenerife in the evening is very impressive. The only time this place gets busy is during the *Fiesta del Charco* (September

Above: A profusion of cacti in Tocodomán.
Right: Luxuriant vegetation near Agaete.

11) and on weekends. The fiesta involves standing in a pond and getting sprayed with water.

Puerto de las Nieves and *Agaete

The road now passes several observation points with fantastic views across the rocky coast and the sea. At the **Mirador del Balcón** (with kiosk) the cliffs fall 400 meters down to the sea below; a little further on, near the observation point of **Andén Verde**, the rocks are even higher. It's worth taking a closer look at the sea through binoculars here – you may see the odd large fish just below the surface.

The small village of **El Risco ⓯** with its *Bar Perdomo* is a good place to refresh yourself before continuing the trip down into the valley. On the sea below you can usually see at least one of the ferry boats that ply between Gran Canaria and Tenerife. They're headed for **Puerto de las Nieves**, the harbor of Agaete (see next page), reached via a left turn just before you reach Agaete. Ever since the ferry connection was established here the place has become busier; beforehand, the only excitement was the fiesta in honor of the *Virgen de las Nieves*. Restaurants serve fresh seafood down by the harbor; the black sand and rocky beaches here and beneath the mountain slope take a bit of getting used to. The steep rock formation known as the **Dedo de Díos** ("Finger of God") is popular with photographers, and is especially attractive when viewed from the harbor.

The most valuable artifact in this town is the triptych in the **Ermita de Nuestra Señora de las Nieves**, possibly the work of the Flemish painter Joos van Cleve (1485-1540), which shows the "Virgin of the Snows" with the infant Jesus at its center. During the festivities celebrating the *Bajada de la Rama* on August 4 each year, a copy is carried in a solemn procession to the main church of Agaete and put on display there. The festival probably

Gran Canaria

dates back to an ancient rain ritual, and includes a water-thrashing ceremony in the harbor as a punishment for lack of rain. It's the perfect way to release frustrations, though whether it's effective is quite another matter.

*Agaete ⑯ is distinctive for its intact center, white houses and narrow alleys. Note the arches on the old bridge across the barranco, and the red cupola on the 19th-century **Iglesia de la Concepción**. Festivals are celebrated in the leafy plaza opposite, otherwise Agaete is a rather sleepy place.

There's a good detour inland at this point; from Ageate to the thermal baths at **Los Berrazales**. The road passes through the Barranco de Agaete with its banana, citrus, mango and avocado plantations, and Los Berrazales can finally be reached via the **Ermita de San Pedro**. The buildings of this former spa are now ruined, but the mineral water can still be used for a cure in the *Princesa Guayarmina* hotel complex. This is just the place to wind down after all that busy sightseeing.

THE MILD NORTH

The northern part of the island is very different from the arid south and the craggy west. Because of its high moisture levels, the north is greener, often cultivated up to high elevations, and dotted with terraced fields. The coastal strip as far as the capital is dominated by plantations and small towns. This high population density has brought a lot of traffic in its wake. Inland things are quieter. The little roads wind their way through the barrancos in hairpin turns, and journeys can take longer than expected. It's worth taking the trouble, however, for the idyllic views across the highly varied mountain and valley scenery.

*Gáldar – Guanche Caves

If you leave Agaete and head in the direction of Gáldar, there's a turnoff to the left (signposted) to the **Reptilandia** reptile park, with over 1,000 turtles, snakes and spiders. Shortly afterwards you'll reach the outskirts of Gáldar. If you feel like visiting a beach or enjoying some seafood, turn off to the left before the center to **Puerto Sardina** ⓱. Six kilometers further on you'll reach a black sand beach in a partly built-up bay. Tourists stray here very rarely – and the restaurants on the beach and in the village serve fresh and very delicious seafood.

The signposted **Necropolis de Gáldar** is easier to find by following the signs in the center of Gáldar rather than through the labyrinth of plantations. It's located between the beach of **El Agujero** and a large banana plantation. Near three structures referred to as mausoleums there are the ruins of some buildings thought to have been the apartments of royal advisors *(guaire)*, the ceremonial hall of the high priest *(faicán)*, and rooms occupied by unmarried holy women *(harimaguadas)*. The necropolis can usually only be inspected from the outside, and there are no regular opening times.

The town of ★**Gáldar** ⓲, on the slopes of the Pico de Gáldar (424 meters), was inhabited as far back as Guanche and Canario times. This is where the kings, known as *guanarteme*, lived in a palace-like structure which later had to make way for a Spanish chapel. The role played by the **Cueva Pintada**, a cave discovered in the town center in 1873, is still unclear. Clay pots and shards were discovered inside it, and are thought to be funerary offerings. There were also several human skeletons. The large geometrical patterns are unusual – there are no comparably well-preserved cave paintings anywhere else on the Canary Islands. The area is closed indefinitely for restoration purposes, unfortunately – but the Museo Canario in Las Palmas contains a copy of a cave wall.

Gáldar is a busy town with a leafy plaza, outside the portals of the mighty

Right: The "flower cheese" (queso de flor) in Guía is mild-tasting.

three-aisled church of **Santiago de los Caballeros** (1778), which – despite its baroque elements – was the first neoclassical structure on the Canaries. It lies above the foundations of an old Canario palace. A green-glazed font dates from the time the islands were conquered by Spain, and the subjugated population was forced to convert to Christianity. The church also contains an organ with a scale of 4,776 different tones. The statues of the *Purisima, Nuestra Señora de la Encarnación, Nuestra Señora del Rosario,* of *Nazareno* and *San Sebastián* are all the work of local master Luján Pérez.

If you take a look inside the inner courtyard of the neoclassical **Ayuntamiento** (Town Hall) on the plaza you'll see a very fine 300-year-old **drago** (dragon tree). The **Casa Museo Antonio Padrón** is in honor of one of the city's sons. The artist Padrón (1920-68) termed himself a "moderate Expressionist," and the museum is worth a trip just to see his strange paintings on Canarian themes.

Santa María de Guía

Santa María de Guía ⓳, a former suburb of Gáldar, has now become a town in its own right. It was here that the most famous and also most prolific of Canarian sculptors, Luján Pérez (1756-1815), grew up. The **Iglesia de la Santa María de Guía** (begun in 1607) in the old part of town here contains many of his works, from the altar painting to various statues of Christ and the Virgin Mary, including *El Crucificado, El Cristo Predicador, El Cristo de la Columna, El Cristo en el Huerto, La Dolorosa* and *Nuestra Señora de las Mercedes*. The whole church is like a private Luján Pérez museum, in fact. The sculptor presented the clock on the right-hand church tower to the local community. On the church facade, a plaque commemorates a famous visitor: the French composer Camille Saint-Saëns (1835-1921), who stayed here at the end

of the 19th century and composed his "Valse Canariote" after hearing some impressive Canarian folk music. He first arrived here incognito, posing as a wine merchant, but a missing persons announcement in a French daily newspaper finally revealed his identity.

Guía is best known for its *queso de flor*, or "flower cheese." Artichoke leaves are used in its preparation. You should definitely visit two excellent cheese shops here: the one by the church (Marqués del Muni 34) and the other right on the main street (Carretera General, near the gas station). The owner, who's been working here since he was a child, also sells honey, rum, tapas and craft items.

If you travel east from Guía in the direction of Las Palmas, a road branches off after three kilometers in the direction of something pleasantly mysterious with a special atmosphere all of its own: the **★Cenobio de Valerón**, a refuge with a rear wall honeycombed with caves. The islands' original inhabitants must have kept a communal granary here under this

rocky overhang, where grain was kept in around 300 different caves. Since there was also a place of assembly *(tagoror)* above the caves, it is assumed that the location must also have had a cultic significance, but as with many Guanche sites, its real purpose remains uncertain. Just take some time to soak in the atmosphere of this strange place.

Moya – Gateway to the Hinterland

Further along the 810 in the direction of the capital you'll cross two very fine bridges – one of them is 125 meters above a barranco and is actually the highest bridge in Spain. Shortly afterwards there's a turnoff southwards into the mountains and to **Moya** ⑳, where the gentle hinterland begins.

The landmark of this village is its church, the **Iglesia El Pilar**, which was built during the 1940s. It majestically dominates the nearby Barranco de Moya. The church contains a *Virgen de la Candelaria* which was brought from

Tenerife to Moya in the 16th century. Opposite the church square is the **Casa Museo Tomás Morales**, inside the birthplace of Modernist poet Tomás Morales (1884-1921). A doctor by profession, he became famous for his collection of poems entitled *Las Rosas de Hercules*. Poetry readings are held regularly in the museum here, attracting the literarily inclined from all over the islands to this rural location.

The once-majestic building housing the former "water exchange" *(Heredad de Aguas de Chorro)* is in a pitiable condition today. In the old days, those who owned water rights were influential and wealthy, and shares in water were attractive investments. The water was here thanks to extensive laurel forests, most of which have now been removed to make way for fields and farmland. You can still see some of the old trees in the **Barranco**

Above: Cenobio de Valerón – a granary and cultic site of the Guanches. Right: The Virgen del Pino with her intriguing face.

de Laurel, south of Moya. If you turn down the high road from Moya to Guía, a narrow mountain road branches off to the left 2.5 kilometers later near **Los Tilos**, heading south into the barranco. Because of the unpaved road, it's better for environmental reasons to drive to (**San Bartolomé de) Fontanales** ㉑ further south, leave the car there and wander up inside the barranco on foot. In the upper part of it you'll cross some fields, and at the bend there's a good view of the laurel forest located further down.

In **Firgas** ㉒, to the east of Moya, a large mineral water company is profiting from the springs in the region. In the town center this source of wealth has been provided with a suitable monument in the shape of the **Paseo de Gran Canaria**. At the center of a promenade leading down a flight of steps, decorated with tiled coats of arms and island maps, a small stream rushes downwards into the valley. At the bottom end of the promenade is a **cultural center**, and the plaza beside it – flanked by the Town Hall and the **Iglesia**

San Roque – is where everyone, young and old, meets up.

From Firgas, a road winds its way southwards up to an elevation of around 900 meters before going back down shortly before the **Balcón de Zamora**, an observation point with a large restaurant, providing a view of Teror and its surrounding landscape from above.

*Teror – Attractive and Historic

With its old-fashioned renovated facades and balconies, *Teror ㉓ is possibly the most attractive village on the island, and its entire center has been listed as protected since 1979. This peaceful little village is the heart of popular religion on Gran Canaria. The *Basílica de Nuestra Señora del Pino (18th century) contains a Madonna figure with an interesting face, one half of which seems to be crying and the other laughing – so it's perfect for the worshipers, who can read anything into it they want. It always seems to show understanding.

Every year on September 7, the *Virgen del Pino* is placed in front of believers under the dome. Before the spectacular robbery of its emeralds in 1975, it was counted among the most valuable Madonna statues in Spain. Strangely enough, the statue is considered so special that it holds the rank of *Capitán General* in the Spanish army – an honor bestowed on it by King Alfonso XIII in 1929 – and because of this, the processions of believers are regularly accompanied by high-ranking soldiers.

The most recent alterations to the appearance of this neoclassical three-aisled basilica date from 1811, when Lúján Pérez changed the western facade. The church is the third to be built on this site. Its octagonal side-tower survives from the previous structure, which was destroyed in a fire. Inside, the gray basalt columns with their honey-brown capitals look very striking. Alongside figures of

Gran Canaria

saints by Luján Pérez the church also contains the five most important rococo paintings on the island, one of which depicts an angel and several believers roasting in purgatory – among them a pope.

A 17th-century townhouse on the central square contains the **Casa Museo Patrones de la Virgen del Pino**. The Manrique de Lara family, the nobles who own the house, have been the custodians of the Virgen del Pino for four generations. The rooms convey a sense of the former elegance of Gran Canarian culture, and the exhibits range from historical photos and paintings to antique furniture and porcelain. The former stables contain saddles and also the state coach of Alfonso XIII, used when he traveled through the island's capital after his coronation in 1906. There is also an English Triumph dating from 1951 on display. The Lower Silesian painter Georg Hedrich (born 1927), who moved to the Canary Islands in 1957 and now lives in Teror, has had a hall of the mu-

seum devoted to his works. His studio, opposite the basilica, is open to visitors.

The small **Plaza Teresa de Bolívar** next to the cathedral is named after the wife of South American freedom fighter Simón Bolívar. It contains a bust of the liberator of the colonies from Spanish domination and also the coat of arms of the Rodríguez del Toro family, from whom his wife was descended. On a raised plaza above the church is the **Episcopal Palace**, with a **cultural center** in one section of it. At the front is the **Town Hall**, which is decorated during festivals.

This whole region is a very good place to go for extensive walks and hikes, and Teror is an ideal starting point for rambles through the surrounding countryside – you can take a detour to the Balcón de Zamora, for instance, or a longer walk to the traditional villages of **Vallesco** and **Lanzarote** off to the west. A more ex-

Above: Teror in festive mood. Right: Well-nourished goats being driven to market at Cardones near Arucas.

hausting hike, which takes a full day to complete, is to go from Teror via Vallesco through the fertile plain to **San Bartolomé de Fontanales**, then from Vallesco to **Valsendero**, and onwards along partially ruined paths in a westerly direction, then downhill through rather varied vegetation, with some excellent views extending as far as the coast. Once you've had a well-deserved rest in Fontanales you can either return by the same route or else continue northwards via **Tablero** and **La Laguna** back into the valley of Teror (3.5 hours each way).

*Arucas – Rum Production Center

Teror produces a mineral water that is famed across the island, and towards the sea in ★**Arucas** ㉔ you can sample some rather strong rum. It is produced by the firm of *Arehucas*, on the outskirts of Banaderos, in the largest rum factory on the archipelago. Around 3.5 million liters of this 90-proof drink are made here each year. The *aguardiente*, thinned down to

around 70 percent alcohol content and less, is kept in 6,000 barrels before being turned into various types of rum. One of the most popular products is the 12-year-old *ron añejo*. The 24-percent *ron miel*, with added honey, is often drunk in place of a liqueur. A **museum** documents the history of rum production in Arucas. You can also see barrels signed by famous visitors, such as the King and Queen of Spain, the Gran Canarian operatic genius Alfredo Kraus, Nobel Peace Prize winner Willy Brandt, artist César Manrique and tenor Plácido Domingo.

Arucas, the third-largest town on the island with a population of 27,000, possesses one of the most unique churches on the archipelago: the ***Iglesia Parroquial de San Juan Bautista**, a massive and yet filigree Neo-Gothic structure made of dark basalt. Its church tower is 60 meters high, making it the tallest in the Canary Islands. A major role in the construction of this church was played by Manuel Vega March, a student of the Catalan architect Antoni Gaudí. The con-

struction of this church extended over decades: it was begun in 1909, consecrated in 1912, completed except for the main tower in 1932, and finally had the main tower finished in 1977. The project received financial support from the owners of the rum factory, the Gourié family, who also bequeathed their former residence to the town, the **Casa del Mayorazgo**, for use as a municipal museum, together with the **Parque Municipal** in front of it.

From Arucas it's worth taking a detour (via a turnoff northwards) to the 412-meter-high **Montaña de Arucas**. Here a **Mirador** provides a fantastic panoramic view, and in the restaurant *El Mesón de la Montaña de Arucas* grown-ups can indulge in excellent food and good wine while their kids romp about in the playground outside.

Leaving Arucas in the direction of the capital, you have two options: the faster route, via the coast road, or the more arduous journey along the 813 parallel to it, which runs through the villages. The coast road leads into the most modern section of La Palma, while the village route reveals the rather less successful side of the city.

LAS PALMAS DE GRAN CANARIA

No other city in the Canary Islands is as metropolitan as **Las Palmas de Gran Canaria** ㉕, which together with Santa Cruz de Tenerife is the capital of the autonomous region. With a population of over 356,000, it is a large harbor city jammed into the rather narrow confines of the northeastern coast, with non-stop real estate construction and several traffic tunnels through the volcanic rock. Las Palmas de Gran Canaria has everything a modern metropolis should have: a historic Old Town with a cathedral, elegant shopping streets, leafy squares, and an exciting cultural life with plenty of museums, galleries and festivals. A shopping trip will take you past attractive emporiums, elegant boutiques and all kinds of other smaller places; there are street cafés and restaurants to relax in and also the magnificent golden-yellow beach of Las Canteras. Alongside all this, however, there are areas of new development with concrete apartment blocks, an area of slums in the outskirts, a drugs scene and also a crime rate that is becoming increasingly disturbing.

Las Palmas de Gran Canaria was founded in 1480 to the south of the Barranco del Guiniguada, which is almost entirely obscured today. The Ermita de San Antonio Abad (see p. 36) still stands at the original location, however. In 1515, Las Palmas was the first community on the Canarian archipelago to be accorded municipal status, and over the decades that followed the San Antón Abad district started to grow. In the 19th century the town began expanding north-

Right: Las Palmas de Gran Canaria – the Canarians' metropolis.

wards rapidly in the direction of La Isleta, and in the 20th century the houses had already started to appear up on the slopes. Access to La Isleta used to be blocked by high tide, and the land had to be reclaimed. The harbor of Puerto de la Luz now lies on the site.

The Old Town Center

Don't bother looking for the city center of Las Palmas de Gran Canaria – because there isn't one. From the La Isleta peninsula, the Canteras beach and modern suburbs in the north, the city extends southwards for kilometers along the sea. The most important sights are in the old center, in the southern part of town. The latter consists of the three districts of **Vegueta**, **Triana** and **Ciudad del Mar**, and you can easily spend a whole day, if not more, exploring their delights.

*Vegueta – Medieval Streets

The most striking building in Vegueta, the oldest section of the city, is the three-aisled cathedral of *Santa Ana ❶. It's much larger than any other church on the Canary Islands – its facade alone measures 100 meters across. The church was started around 1500, and the dark-gray late-Gothic basalt columns along the nave are part of the original structure. In 1599, the capital was plundered and burned by the Dutch pirate Van der Does and his men; they stole all the icons and pictures from the cathedral, and destroyed the choir and pulpit. Since they also burned the entire cathedral archives, very little is now known of the building's early history. Santa Ana owes its present-day appearance to alteration work that lasted from 1852 into the 20th century. The neoclassical facade, with its arched portal, rose window, stone baldachin above the central section and two towers (the left of which is a belfry as well as a clock tower) all date from that time.

Gran Canaria

Renovation of the entire interior was completed in 1998, and the difference is remarkable: the once rather dimly-lit interior is now flooded with light, and the cathedral has gained a new and special magnificence. A section on the north side is due to be turned into a sanctuary. On the south side of the cathedral is the *Patio de los Naranjos*, a courtyard of orange trees, which can be admired during a visit to the Museo Diocesano de Arte Sacro – the courtyard is pleasantly shady, and also makes the whole place somewhat reminiscent of Seville.

The interior of the cathedral has side-chapels off to the left and right, and the side aisles are separated from the central nave by impressive, 20-meter-high rows of pillars. The side-chapels contain the tombs of several bishops, as well as of the first proper chronicler of Canarian history, José Viera y Clavijo, the poet Bartolomé Cairasco de Figueroa, and the politician Fernando León y Castillo. Beneath the dome, on the crossing, there are 16 larger-than-life wooden statues of saints, all painted gray to make them look like stone. These are the work of sculptor and architect Luján Pérez, who also made the changes to the facade during the 19th century. More of his works can be admired in the side-chapels, including a *Redeemer* and the *Virgen de la Antigua*.

The most impressive works by Luján Pérez are inside the **Museo Diocesano de Arte Sacro** (the entrance to which is at Calle Espiritu Santo 20), located in the southern part of the cathedral complex. Five halls contain religious works by various artists, and in the chapter hall on the first floor you can see Luján's deeply moving *Dolorosa*. It is carried through the streets of Las Palmas every Easter, together with a statue of Christ (also by Luján). The floor of the chapter hall is covered with hand-made ceramic tiles; the only mosaic of its type anywhere in the Canary Islands.

The large, slightly sloping **Plaza de Santa Ana** ❷ in front of the cathedral is surrounded by attractive townhouses and several historic structures. The cast-iron

black dogs on the eastern side of the square, directly opposite the cathedral facade, are a popular meeting point. These dogs are meant to be reminders of how the Canary Islands got their name: according to Roman historians, large dogs had apparently been found on newly-discovered islands in the eastern Atlantic. Whether the name "Canary" really comes from *canis*, the Latin word for dog, or whether it is derived from the name of a Berber tribe (as claimed by the author James Krüss, who died in 1997) is still a subject of some controversy.

Cross over to the north side of the square and admire the monastery-like **Episcopal Palace**, built in the Renaissance style in 1630. It's still in use today and so, unfortunately, is closed to visitors. Beside it is the impressive 16th-century **Casa del Regente**, with its Renaissance facade. Once the seat of the Spanish governor, it houses the law courts today.

On the south side of the square there are several other buildings, some with Art

Nouveau ornamentation. The chronicler José Viera y Clavijo lived and also died in one of them (marked with a plaque on the facade), and today the building houses the **Archivo Histórico Provincial**, where scientists can inspect private and official documents about population censuses, land sales, water rights, the slave trade, goods transportation and numerous other archives.

On the western side of the square, opposite the cathedral facade, is the neoclassical building that was once the **Ayuntamiento**, or Town Hall. It stands on the site of the former Town Hall, which burned down in 1842, and has now grown too small as well.

To the south of the plaza, between the Town Hall and the cathedral, on Calle del Doctor Chil, there is a triangular square with the **Fuente del Espíritu Santo ❸** at its center. This wonderful neoclassical fountain was created by Manuel Oraa. Next to it, in the simple chapel of **Ermita del Espíritu Santo**, services were once held for Africans who had been brought

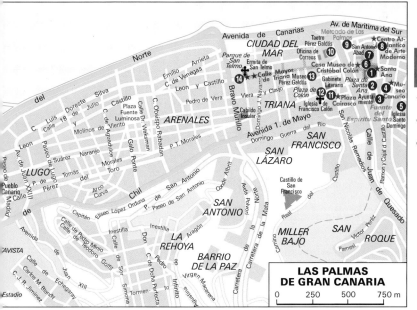

here to do forced labor during the days of slavery.

On Calle del Doctor Chil (on the corner of Calle Verneau), the excellent ***Museo Canario** ❹ contains important finds from the pre-Hispanic era, including mummies with the grave goods interred alongside them, and also a collection of skulls with a list of the various recognizable diseases, injuries or operations their former owners once had; among the exhibits you can also see a reconstruction of the Cueva Pintada in Gáldar, along with items of jewelry, idols, clay stamps, ceramics, weapons and tools. A library with a large selection of archeological and ethnographic literature is also available. The museum, based on the collection of the doctor Gregorio Chil y Naranjo, is financed by a private foundation and is the oldest in the city. Naranjo started the collection in 1880 before bequeathing the building and all the scientific documentation inside it to Las Palmas. The museum is certainly worth spending a few hours in, and gives a good

insight into the history of the islands before the Spanish arrived.

A detour southwards via Calle Agustín Millares leads to the shady **Plaza Santo Domingo**. This is where the conqueror Pedro de Vera once had a country estate with a sugar-cane plantation. The **Iglesia Santo Domingo** ❺ (early 16th century) survived the fire attack by Dutch pirates and still contains a fine baroque altar, as well as works by Luján Pérez and one of his pupils, Fernando Estévez. The latter created the *Virgen del Rosario*, and works here by Luján Pérez include the statue of Christ in the side altar. The square outside the church was where non-believers were burned at the stake, and is still familiarly known as the *Plaza de la Quemada*, or "Square of the Burned."

Behind the cathedral to the east stands the ***Casa Museo de Cristóbal Colón** ❻ (Calle Colón 1), with its impressive, richly ornamented Gothic portal, finely carved balconies and leafy inner courtyard. The museum is entered through a side door. According to legend, Christo-

pher Columbus stayed in this imposing building while two of his three caravels were being repaired. The fascinating museum deals with topics such as pre-Hispanic America, the life and times of Christopher Columbus, the situation of the Canary Islands between continents, and the development of the city of Las Palmas. There is a very fine reconstruction of Columbus's cabin on board the *Santa Maria*, and it gives a good impression of what life must have been like at sea in those days. Another department contains some excellent etchings and paintings from the Prado Museum in Madrid, including several works by Francisco Goya.

The chapel **Ermita de San Antonio Abad** ❼ (see also p. 32) a short distance further away to the northeast was completed at the end of the 15th century and

Above: The Casa Museo de Cristóbal Colón is a jewel of Canarian architecture. Right: The Mercado de Las Palmas – a landmark of the capital.

renovated in the 18th century. According to legend, this is where Columbus is supposed to have prayed to God that his venture would succeed.

Further south is Calle de los Balcones. Modern art and architecture have found an impressive new home in a converted townhouse on this street: the ***Centro Atlántico de Arte Moderno (CAAM)** ❽ presents alternating exhibitions on a variety of themes, mainly with an emphasis on the cultural situation of Gran Canaria between the continents of Europe, Africa and the Americas. A permanent modern art exhibition is planned for the building next door. The rooftop terrace of this ultra-modern and functional building provides a pleasantly romantic view of the cathedral and the houses of the Old Town.

After all this art and history it's a good idea to take a well-deserved break in the roofed-over **Mercado de Las Palmas** ❾, on the northeastern corner of Vegueta. This is the oldest market hall in the city, and is a paradise of sights, sounds and

smells. If you want to buy any fresh seafood, this is the place to come.

★Triana – Bourgeois Magnificence

The suburb of ★**Triana**, with its numerous small stores and boutiques, begins to the north of the Juan de Quesada highway. In contrast to the rather feudal-looking Vegueta with all its alleyways and old buildings, the Triana quarter is extremely varied. Formerly inhabited by Andalusian, English, Maltese and Danish merchants, it has much less homogeneous architecture; in fact, almost every architectural style of the 19th and 20th centuries, including postmodernism, can be found here. This variety makes the whole area quite fascinating, however, and it's interesting just to stroll past the different buildings and guess their architectural styles.

From the market hall in the Vegueta quarter, cross the main road towards the outwardly rather dusty-looking **Teatro Pérez Galdós** ⓾. The building was first named after the Spanish dramatist Tirso de Molina in 1888, but it was destroyed by a fire in 1918. After its reconstruction the theater received its new name in honor of writer and dramatist Benito Pérez Galdós (1843-1920), a native of the city who spent the first 19 years of his life here. He became famous for his cycle of romances, *Episodios Nacionales*, in which he painted a fascinating portrait of the morals of his time.

The theater building was reconstructed under the supervision of architect Miguel Martín Fernández de la Torre. He got his brother, Nestor de la Torre, a famous artist and stage designer, to decorate the rooms with drawings, paintings and wood carvings. Part of the building is dedicated to the French composer Camille Saint-Saëns, who stayed on Gran Canaria incognito and, to everyone's surprise, commented expertly on the rehearsals of the local philharmonic orchestra (see also pp. 26-27).

One of the most pleasant squares in this quarter of the city is the ★**Plaza Cairasco**

literary salon, and locals refer to it as the *Casino*. Only members have access, and visitors are merely allowed to peek inside the roofed-over inner courtyard. The brief glimpse of the large staircase and three-storied arcades is definitely worth the trouble, however.

On the raised **Plaza de Colón** ⑫ there is the **Busto a Colón**, a pillar bearing a bust of the great explorer Columbus. The long church behind it is the three-aisled **Iglesia de San Francisco de Asís** (17th century). Alongside a floor made of white Carrara marble and the typical *mudéjar* ceiling, it also contains two important statues by Luján Pérez: one of St. John and also a *Señor del Huerto*. The *Virgen de la Soledad* here is also interesting from an art historical point of view: some experts believe her features are the same as those of Isabella of Castile, the founder of the church.

Calle de los Malteses leads to the **Museo Pérez Galdós** ⑬ on Calle Cano. This almost cute little birthplace of the famous author contains a selection of memorabilia of his life – from his cradle to his deathbed to his death mask. Items of furniture designed by Galdós from his apartment in Madrid and his bedroom can also be seen here. A library contains original copies of his works as well as translations, correspondence and scientific papers.

The main destination of this stroll is the ****Calle Mayor de Triana** ⑭, because the renovated facades of the buildings here are true masterpieces. The Art Nouveau buildings also have several contemporary elements – from the optician to the bank, and from the boutique to the fast food outlet. There's a pleasant leafy café at the end of the pedestrian precinct in the **Parque de San Telmo**. You sit in a pavilion filled with colorful tiles, the ***Quiosco Modernista** of Valencian architect Rafael Masanet Fau. It's worth coming to the park for this little jewel alone. The late baroque **Ermita de San**

⑪, named after the poet Bartolomé Cairasco de Figueroa. Its charm derives mainly from two important buildings: the **Gabinete Literario** and also the **Hotel Madrid**, where General Franco stayed on July 17, 1936, at the beginning of the Spanish Civil War, determined to undertake a military putsch against the lawfully elected government of the Republic. He flew from here to Morocco in a private English plane and then took over as supreme commander for the attack on the motherland. The bar on the ground floor of the hotel has tables outside in the palm-lined square.

The Gabinete Literario was originally the Teatro Cairasco, but the latter soon proved to be too small. In 1884, the graceful stuccoed house with its little towers and balconies thus became a cross between a private gentlemen's club and a

Above: African traders are a part of the scene. Right: Spanish Art Nouveau pavilion in the Parque de San Telmo – a good place for an extended coffee break.

Telmo chapel at the western corner of the park is consecrated to the patron saint of fishermen, as is evident from the many votive pictures inside. To the east of the park, on Avenida Rafael Cabrera, is the bus station **Estación de Guaguas**.

Ciudad del Mar and Pueblo Canario

It's a lot more modern altogether in **Ciudad del Mar**, because parts of the terrain around here were only reclaimed from the sea as recently as the 1960s. The narrow strip between the coastal highway and the Triana quarter is packed with tall administrative tower blocks and corporate buildings.

To the north of the Triana quarter and of Ciudad del Mar are the less attractive suburbs of **Arenales** and **Lugo**. Cross over to the villa district of **Ciudad Jardín** in the **Parque Doramas** and you'll find the **Pueblo Canario** ⓯. This ensemble of buildings has been designed as a modern interpretation of traditional Canarian architecture. There are stores selling art and craft items and souvenirs, a café and a tourist information center. On Thursday afternoons and Sunday mornings there are folklore performances held here. Otherwise, the patio is a popular place for celebrations and marriages.

A key role in the creation of the Pueblo Canario was played by Gran Canarian artist Néstor de la Torre (1887-1938), who with amazing foresight was predicting tourism as the future role of the Canaries as long ago as 1934. Like César Manrique later on, he wanted to preserve the islands' cultural identity and independence. The small but excellent ***Museo Néstor** is dedicated to his attitude to art and his own works. It contains an exquisite selection of the incredible amount of material this highly versatile artist produced.

Alongside several of his early works there are also sections from his painting cycle entitled *El Poema del Atlántico* on

display. His interests ranged from folkwear and costume design to stage design, and also construction plans for tourist facilities.

A further highlight of his creative output is the unfinished cycle of paintings *El Poema de la Tierra*, in which he embeds the erotic shapes of two lovers inside the exotic forms of plants native to the Canary Islands. Néstor de la Torre is seen as an exponent of *Modernismo* (an art movement in Spain influenced by the French Romantics and Symbolists).

The Parque Doramas was originally the grounds of the Hotel Santa Catalina, one of the best in the city (which includes a casino). The park is rather neglected now, but contains several modern statues illustrating the history of the Guanches. Nearby are a swimming pool and also a tennis club.

The elegant side of Las Palmas opens up in the boutiques and sophisticated department stores on Avenida de José Mesa y López, on the northern edge of the district of **Alcaravaneras**. The presence of

department store giant *El Corte Inglés* is very obvious, with its two buildings on either side of the tree-lined avenue. This is where you'll sometimes see limousines with liveried chauffeurs taking diplomats and their wives out to shop. Unless you're feeling especially rich, it's probably a good idea to keep your wallet closed around here.

Santa Catalina and the Harbor District

The clientele in the bars and restaurants is quite colorful in the streets and squares of the **Santa Catalina** district, located between the harbor to the east and the municipal beach of Las Canteras to the west. The heart of this area is the large green square known as ***Parque de Santa Catalina** ⑯. Couples, sailors, old-age pensioners and tradesmen walk along

Above: Life's a game in the Parque de Santa Catalina. Right: The Playa de Las Canteras is the city's Copacabana.

here past the souvenir shops, bars and newsstands; tourists collect information material from the **Casa de Tourismo**, and the *aficionados* of dominoes, chess and cards all play their games here. This whole area is busy at the best of times, but becomes astonishingly active when the annual carnival reaches its climax.

The harbor of **Puerto de la Luz** ⑰, completed as a means of creating employment at the end of the 19th century, is considered the largest in Spain. It is now the most important container shipping port in the North African region. The yacht harbor bordering it to the south attracts plenty of sailors eager to participate in the international transatlantic regattas.

In the old days the harbor, and the ships lying here at anchor, had to be protected from attack from British, French and Dutch pirates, who were usually sent here by their monarchs and had some very powerful fleets. The mighty defensive bulwark in such situations was the **Castillo de la Luz** ⑱, on the south bank of the **La Isleta** peninsula, which was

Gran Canaria

built above the foundations of a fort dating from the days of the *Conquista* and had 11 batteries. The fort failed to withstand the attack in 1599 by the pirate Pieter van der Does, with his 84 ships, and was completely razed to the ground. Today it is used for cultural purposes. A word of warning, by the way: Avoid the park area beside it, which has now become a center of the drug scene. The streets north of the fort are hectic and businesslike: between the bars and bodegas, various shipping and trading companies have established themselves, and Calle de Juan Rejón contains numerous Indian and Chinese shops with a whole range of exotic goods for sale. There are even shops tailored to the special requirements of Russian sailors.

Near the harbor, the bars generally cater to the many mariners who visit here regularly, and the whole area is reasonably seedy: there are snack bars here, fast food outlets, and also traditional tapas bars, closely followed by dubious-looking nightclubs and sex shops. Near

the *Playa de Las Canteras* ⓭ things get slightly better, with several good restaurants and cafés.

The yellow sand beach, protected by a rocky reef from the sea, is one of the most popular on the island. During the week it is reasonably full, but on weekends all the Palmeros come here with their extended families and have a relaxed beach holiday weekend, which can involve anything from a simple picnic to a small-scale soccer tournament. There is a sailing school here, too, teaching young people in small boats.

On the beach promenade, street cafés and restaurants with terraces of all different kinds lie one beside the next, from the *Cafetería Mozart* – a popular meeting place for local families – to the elegant restaurant in the five-star *Reina Isabel* hotel, and also the American-style *Off Shore*, where young people gather in the evenings to drink tropical cocktails and listen to English crooners.

If you feel like combining a visit to a **flea market** with a visit to the beach and the restaurant and bar area beyond it, it's best to visit Santa Catalina on a Sunday morning: near the city highway, behind the hotel tower of Los Bardinos and almost as far as the Castillo de la Luz, you'll find all kinds of junk, artistic and otherwise, on sale. It's easy to spend several hours here without noticing how the time goes by – and the prices are often very reasonable, too, which of course adds to the enjoyment. Beware of pickpockets, by the way – flea markets are a favorite haunt of theirs.

In the southwest, beyond the Paseo de las Canteras, a new business district has appeared with several shopping centers. This is where you'll find a building that has become the talking point of the classical music fraternity ever since it was opened in December 1997: the **★★Auditorio Alfredo Kraus** ⓴, a modern palace made of massive natural stone, which was designed by the Catalan architect Óscar Tusquet. Leading international orchestras, soloists and conductors all perform here – indeed the building has done an enormous amount to enhance the quality of classical music in the Canaries, and has placed Las Palmas de Gran Canaria on a par with many other leading musical locations in the world.

The special architectural feature here is that the back of the stage in the main concert hall provides a view of the sea – a unique feature which makes for regularly inspiring performances. This building, with its total of 10 concert halls, represents the fulfillment of a lifetime dream for opera star Alfredo Kraus, and is now the city's top cultural address. Make sure you fit attending at least one concert here into your itinerary.

Near the Auditorio you'll reach the municipal highway, westbound section, with a **rock statue** by Tony Gallardo dedicated to the lost continent of Atlantis.

Right: Tafira Alta with its Italian-style manor houses.

THE ARID EAST

Tafira

For a detour inland, take the coast highway heading south, following the turnoff to Tafira while still inside the capital; it leads between the districts of Vegueta and Triana and into the mountains. After several hairpin bends you'll arrive in **Tafira Baja** ⓶, which has developed into a kind of suburb for wealthy commuters. The streets here all have suitably opulent-looking villas along them. At the entrance to the town is the **University of Gran Canaria**, founded in 1989. It was built in a simple neoclassical style, but also has a few Bauhaus elements to it.

One special highlight of Tafira Baja is the **★Jardín Botánico Canario Viera y Clavijo**. You can already hear the birds singing as you park your car. From the restaurant and from an observation platform there's a good view of the area. Most of this botanical garden was laid out on the steep wall of a barranco, with surfaced footpaths and cascades leading past it in the direction of the valley. The main attraction featured here is the flora of the archipelago: each Canarian plant species has its own little reserve, even the Canarian laurel forest; and there are also lots of different kinds of succulents for cactus aficionados.

Tafira Alta ⓷, which adjoins the garden to the southwest, is distinctive for its mainly Italian-style villas with their magnificent gardens, terraces and verandas. If the through traffic weren't so noisy and irritating it would be nice to take a leisurely stroll past these fine buildings. A very striking one is the **Villa María**, built in the Andalusian-Moorish style and right next to the main road.

At the end of the village the road bends away in the direction of the **Caldera de Bandama**. It passes through vineyards, where the popular *Vino del Monte* grows. The winding road also passes several

Gran Canaria

wine estates before it reaches the famous Bandama Crater (569 meters), which is 200 meters deep. A farmer is still tilling fields right at its base. From an observation point above the Caldera you can see the coastal strip from La Isleta beyond Las Palmas all the way to the airport. To the west of the crater there is a golf course.

*Telde – Traces of the Guanches

To reach Telde, it's best to go back up the main road to Tafira Alta and carry on towards Las Palmas from there until you reach a right turn (easy to miss) that will take you to **Marzagán**. The narrow, winding side road leads past vineyards and, just before Marzagán, goes by the hemispherical building housing the American School of Gran Canaria. Next you'll pass the weird concrete jungle of **Jinámar**, with its tedious apartment buildings lined up one after the other against the hilly landscape. Since this place has the same social problems as

other similar areas all over the world, attempts are being made to offer a comprehensive cultural program – but the people who usually attend the events come here from the city center.

★**Telde ㉘** – in pleasant contrast to Jinámar – possesses a historic center. To look at this place it's hard to believe that it has a population of around 90,000. Across to the right, beyond the valley, the picturesque suburb of San Francisco is huddled around the church of the same name, and can be reached by a footpath from the plaza at the Basílica San Juan Bautista that leads across an old aqueduct. The streets of San Francisco are cobbled with dark-gray, oval basalt stones, and here you can still see the old, dark street signs which have been replaced by more modern, Guanche-ornamented ones nearly everywhere else.

To the left is the broad square in front of the **Basílica San Juan Bautista**. This church contains a Gothic altarpiece from Flanders with six scenes from the life of the Virgin Mary, a statue of John the Bap-

tist by Fernando Estévez from Orotava (Tenerife), and a statue of the martyr *San Pedro de Verona* by Luján Pérez. The baptismal chapel contains a font of Carrara marble and also frescoes by Gran Canarian artist Jesús González Arenciba, painted in 1948. The crucified Christ at the main altar is a bizarre work by Mexican Indios. Because the 1.85-meter-high statue was made from maize paste, it only weighs seven kilograms. The color of Jesus's face changes with the seasons, a fact ascribed to a wood-stain derived from seeds. Beyond the church, on the left, a promenade leads to the **historical archives** and to the **public library**. There's a choice of cafés on the plaza in front of the **Iglesia San Gregorio**.

By the way, don't miss a visit to the **Casa Museo León y Castillo**, which can be reached from the church square by fol-

Above: Replica of the "Idol of Tara" in the church square of Ingenio. Right: Hem-stitch embroidery – a local specialty (Museo de Piedras y Artesanía, Ingenio).

lowing the main street. The museum contains the estate of the diplomat Fernando León y Castillo, which ranges from a collection of walking sticks to a Paris Opera ticket, and also a collection of Impressionist and contemporary paintings. It's quite astonishing what he managed to collect, and the exhibits provide a fascinating insight into what life was like during the late 19th and early 20th centuries.

Telde is definitely historic ground, as proven by old documents. The Italian fortress builder Leonardo Torriani claims in his 16th-century report that he counted 14,000 Guanche houses here. The Guanche symbolic figure known as the *Idolo de Tara* was found in the part of town called **Tara**: the torso of a clay figure with noticeably thick upper arms and thighs. The figure is on display in the Museo Canario in the capital, and copies of it are popular souvenirs.

Most of the archeological sites in this section are in appalling condition, and to get a proper sense of the history of this region it's best to visit the area called **Cuatro Puertas** south of town, roughly halfway towards Ingenio. On a hill that was sacred to the Guanches, you'll see a former "residential cave" with four door openings. If you cross around from the cave, which is on the shady side of the hill, to the sunny side, you'll find further relics from Guanche times, including a complex of caves and also a piece of rock with carvings that is thought to have once formed part of a sacrificial altar. This place is very atmospheric, especially around dusk.

Ingenio, Agüimes, Arinaga

The name **Ingenio** ㉙ ("Sugar Mill") indicates the former importance of this place for the sugar-cane industry. The **Museo de Piedras y Artesanía** in the suburb of **Mejías** is actually a sales exhibition of Canarian arts and crafts. In the entrance area there's a collection of stones on display, and you can also watch women as they embroider. The chapel at the center of the complex is jam-packed with devotional material; its prominent visitors included Maria Callas (1967) with the Greek shipowner Aristotle Onassis. In the part of town called **Las Rosas**, across to the east in the direction of the highway, a former manor house contains a similar exhibition of crafts for sale. An old mill can also be seen there.

There's a generously-sized church square at the center of Ingenio. The church itself, with its two towers and white dome, can be seen far and wide, and it houses the statue of the patron saint of the Canary Islands, the *Virgen de la Candelaria*. Beneath the church, a copy of the *Idolo de Tara* has been set up. Many of the house walls have large-sized pictures of village scenes on them, and there is also some Guanche ceramic ornamentation on several buildings. At the eastern end of the village in the direction of Carrizal, someone has placed an full-scale model of a sugar mill in the middle of a traffic island.

The central church of **Agüimes ㉚** also clearly dominates the town, with its pastel-colored houses up on the steep slope of the Barranco de Guayadeque. The buildings are all closely huddled together, and together with the narrow streets give the place a distinctly medieval look. The three-aisled **Parroquía San Sebastián**, declared a "historic cultural monument of Spain," contains three statues by Luján Pérez: a *Virgen de la Esperanza*, a *Santo Domingo* and a *San Vincente*.

The entrance to the village of Agüimes marks the start of the always green **∗Barranco de Guayadeque**, which was one of the most populated places on the island in former days. The road winds its way along the bed of the (largely dried-out) stream at the bottom of the ravine, and up into the hinterland. You won't only see caves dating from the Guanche period here – some modern cave dwell-

Gran Canaria

ings and also a chapel have been cut out of the rock as well. The main attraction here, however, is the regular series of folklore performances held in the caves. Busloads of tourists arrive here for them all the time. The nicest time of day in the barranco is the peaceful period just after sunrise, because carousing tends to go on until very late at night here.

If you travel from the Agüimes plateau down to Arinaga, you'll see nothing but modern buildings stretching away to the south. **Arinaga ㉛**, beside the sea, looks half-finished in several places, but tourism should soon transform it into yet another holiday paradise. The sandy beach, with its promenade, faces the sea in a half-moon shape. The sunny spots of the south can be reached very quickly via the nearby highway.

HIGHLIGHTS OF THE INTERIOR

The center of Gran Canaria contains the most spectacular mountain ranges anywhere on the island. Striking mono-

liths and rock formations rear up out of volcanic cones and mountain ridges into the azure-blue sky. As a rule these are volcanic vents that have withstood erosion for millions of years. Looking at them, it's easy to understand why the Guanches worshiped these storm and rain-lashed shapes as gods. There are new and even more breathtaking views at each bend in the road, and it's hard to understand why many people who have never visited Gran Canaria automatically assume that the scenery here has nothing very special about it, and that the whole island is covered with tourist areas.

The table mountains and plateaus up here have corn growing on them; it gets turned into *gofio* (roast flour; see p. 74), and is supposed to give the Canarios (what they claim is) their immense strength. Between the cornfields you can also see the odd cabbage and vegetable

Above: Donkeys and mules are still used in the mountains. Right: Artenara – old caves, new accommodation.

patch which the locals cultivate for their own use. The dry seasons are successfully bridged with the help of several reservoirs located nearby.

If you leave Las Palmas in the direction of Tafira, you'll reach a historic section of mountain ridge just after you've passed through Tafira Alta. On the **Monte Lentiscal** the Dutch pirate Pieter van der Does had to abandon his plan to subjugate the entire island: with his 4,000-man troop he was beaten back by a courageous horde of just 500 militiamen. In nearby **Santa Brígida ㉜** this event is celebrated with a special festival (ask about dates and times at the local tourist information center). The village lies 500 meters up, and is perhaps the most exclusive residential area near the island's capital. It was valued for its slightly cool climate at the turn of the century, mainly by wealthy English visitors who used it as a summer spa. Outside the old center there are several neoclassical and postmodern villas inside leafy grounds. Breathing the fresh air here after the heat of the beaches makes one wonder whether tourism may soon concentrate more on health and relaxation rather than on suntans and sand. Then again, judging from the age and elegance of the houses here, it's pretty easy to tell what has lasting importance in the long run.

The road rises another 300 meters to reach the rather modern-looking village of **Vega de San Mateo ㉝**, an agricultural center with regular cattle markets. This water-rich high valley contains not only fruit and vegetables, but also special herbs used in traditional medicines. Shortly after you enter the village, Canarian entrepreneur Jesús Gómez has created the **Casa Museo Cho' Zacarias** on his estate, some parts of which are 300 years old. The exhibition documents the traditional, fast-vanishing everyday culture of the island world. Since there is also a very good restaurant here, be prepared for a crush at weekends.

While the high valley of **Las Lagunetas** still looks reasonably cultivated, you'll soon notice that the landscape gets very rough and barren as you approach the rocky heights of the central Caldera Massif. The next place you reach is the **Cruz de Tejeda** ㉞, a stone cross, around which restaurants, souvenir shops, children's donkey rides and a country hotel have all sprung up. If you're traveling with kids, this is a good place to distract them. From the *Parador Nacional* on the edge of the crater (closed for overnight stays at present) and from various other locations close by you'll get magnificent views of the mountains and valleys of Gran Canaria. By the way, if you don't like having a lot of people around, it's best to avoid this place on weekends.

To get to know the volcanism on Gran Canaria from another angle, travel from here in a northwesterly direction to the **Pinos de Gáldar** ㉟. From an observation point you can look down into a crater full of reddish and black volcanic ash. You'd think there had been a recent eruption if it weren't for the green foliage all around. The crater was formed at least 3,000 years ago, when the island was still relatively uninhabited.

Now we're approaching the region of Canaria where numerous cave dwellings from the pre-Christian era are still in use. From a long way off you'll already notice ★**Artenara** ㊱: a statue of Jesus reminiscent of the one in Rio de Janeiro welcomes visitors with its arms outstretched. This is the highest village on Gran Canaria (1,250 meters) and in the surrounding hamlets as far as Juncalillo and beyond, people have built dwellings and granaries, but also churches and chapels underground.

A short cobbled path for pilgrims leads eastwards from the village center to a cave chapel, where the shrine of the *Virgen de la Cuevita* has been carved from the reddish-brown tuff. West of the village, a pedestrian tunnel leads to the *Méson La Silla* restaurant, where you can eat on a terrace and enjoy a magnificent

view of the mountain scenery at the same time.

From Artenara, even in bad weather, it's worth taking a detour to the largest intact forest area on the island, the nature reserve of the **★Pinar de Tamadaba**, 12 kilometers to the west. A paved road leads around the Tamadaba Massif (1,444 meters), affording impressive views of the Caldera de Tejeda, the coast in the west and also of Tenerife with Teide. In foggy weather the pine forest is transformed into something straight out of a fairy tale. The whole place is extremely mysterious: enormous chunks of rock lie strewn among the trees, and water glistens on the greenish-yellow lianas that hang from the branches. The forest is an ideal place to go for a hike or a picnic. Spending the night in the idyllically-located camp and picnic site in the north-

Above: Mountain-bikers in the "petrified storm" (Miguel de Unamuno). Right: The monumental beauty of barren mountain scenery south of Karge Fataga.

west is free of charge, but no services are provided apart from a water supply. Travel back by car from the Pinar de Tamadaba in the direction of Artenara. A few kilometers outside the town a winding road branches off to the west, in the direction of Acusa and San Nicolás de Tolentino, which are among the highlights of any island tour (see p. 22 ff.).

If the road from Artenara to **Tejeda** ❸ has become impassable – and this often happens after rockfalls caused by rain – you'll have no choice but to make a detour via Pinos de Gáldar and Cruz de Tejeda. Surrounded by terraced fields of corn, and fruit and vegetable fields, Tejeda is located 1,000 meters up on the slopes of the enormous crater of the same name. Without the tourist boom this place would have been deserted long ago, because surviving from agriculture in this barren landscape is very difficult. Around 50 percent of the villagers have turned their backs on this place in the past.

A few kilometers further on in the direction of San Bartolomé de Tirajana, a

road branches off to the ***Roque Bentayga** (1,404 meters). This basalt cliff is
part of the **Parque Arquéologico del
Bentayga**, which provides information
on archeological finds and sites in the region. Signposted hiking routes, providing
views into the neighboring barrancos,
lead to a series of caves that also includes
the great **Cueva del Rey**, or the "King's
Cave."

If you follow the 815 further southwards, you'll arrive in the small town of
Ayacata ❸. Here the access road to the
*Roque Nublo (1,817 meters) – the most
famous landmark on the island –
branches off towards the northeast. A
good, well-marked hiking route starts at a
parking lot beside the road and winds its
way up to the "Cloud Rock." Several bro-
ken boulders, cracked by erosion, lie
strewn across the slopes; these once
formed part of the massif, and all that remains of it now are the Roque Nublo and
several smaller rocky fingers, such as **El
Fraile** ("The Monk") further to the south.
The names go well with the rocks, and if

you stare long enough at El Fraile it really
does look like a monk.

From Ayacata you can take a nice detour to the highest mountain on the island,
the **Pico de las Nieves** (1,949 meters). In
the car, follow the road past the Roque
Nublo and turn southeast at the next inter-
section near Cruz Llanos de la Paz; a few
kilometers later a road branches off to the
right through pine forests to the summit,
which can also be reached on foot. A picnic area has been built here, and from the
observation point you can see the southwest of the island with the neighboring
Caldera de Tirajana crater.

From Pico de las Nieves you can either
continue on to Telde and Teror, or drive
back to Ayacata. From there, a winding
stretch of road leads on to Mogán and to
the southwest coast (see p. 22). If you de-
cide to take the 815 southwards from
Ayacata, you can go via the pass of **Cruz
Grande** to **San Bartolomé de Tirajana
❸**. The **church** in this town contains folk
art: on the right of the altar there are two
equestrian statues, showing St. Jacob

(*Santiago*) triumphing over the "heathen" Moors: one of them is large and aggressive-looking, the other small and rather naively done.

Just after San Bartolomé de Tirajana the road makes a fork: a scenically attractive stretch of road leads off southwards via the picturesquely situated town of **Fataga ㊵**, and then on to the coast and Playa del Inglés. The landscape around here becomes very monumental yet again, with broad barrancos and massive, barren mountain ridges. To really appreciate the scenery, and especially if you have kids in tow, try visiting one of the three camel stations here, which provide rides through this astonishing, desert-like region, with its handful of palm-lined oases. Camel riding isn't that difficult, and it's a very memorable experience.

If you go left at the fork in the road you'll arrive in **Santa Lucía ㊶**, where the white church with its dome looks rather like a mosque when seen from a distance. Near the *Restaurante Hao*, a castle-like structure contains the private **Museo del Castillo de la Fortaleza**, in which archeological finds from the surrounding area are on display. Around one kilometer to the south of the village, a right turn leads to the palm forest of **La Sorrueda ㊷** and to a historically important rocky ridge. This was the former site of the Guanche mountain fortress of *Alsite*, renamed **Fortaleza Grande** by the Spanish. It was here that the Guanches made their last stand, until they were finally forced to surrender; two of their leaders jumped from the rocks to their deaths. On April 29 each year a ceremony is held on the plateau behind the fortress in honor of them. Access to the coastal highway is very fast from here, via Agüimes. After this tour into the interior with its stunning scenery it's rather difficult to believe the common misconception about Gran Canaria being an island destroyed and made ugly by touristic development.

GRAN CANARIA

ARRIVAL: By Plane: The *Aeropuerto de Gando* is 22 kilometers south of the capital, tel. 928-579000. Tourist information, rental cars, currency exchange. Bus transfer every 20 minutes.
By Ship: *Transmediterránea*, tel. 928-260070, feries several times a week to and from Tenerife, jetfoil several times a day. *Naviera Armas*, tel. 928-474080, ferries to and from Tenerife, Lanzarote, Fuerteventura.
By Bus: Bus terminal *Estación de Guaguas*, opposite the Parque de San Telmo, Avda. Rafael Cabrera. It's very useful to have a working knowledge of Spanish here. The firm for the capital and the southeast is "Salcai," tel. 928-381110, and "Utinsa" does the capital and the northwest, tel. 928-360179.

THE SOUTH

MASPALOMAS AND ENVIRONS
⊛⊛⊛ Hotel Maspalomas Oasis, Avda. del Oasis, tel. 928-141448, fax. 928-141192. The most luxurious hotel on the island, with a park right next to the dunes; **Helga Masthoff Park and Sport Hotel Los Palmitos**, Barranco de los Palmitos (above the Parque Palmitos), tel. 928-142100, fax. 928-141114. Gardens, tennis, golf, pool, excellent restaurant.
Restaurante Amaiur, Avda. Neckermann 42, tel. 928-764414. Next to the golf course, Basque fish specialties, good wines, desserts closed Sundays; **Restaurante Orangerie**, Avda. del Oasis, tel. 928-140806. Excellent restaurant in the Hotel Maspalomas Oasis, modern Canarian cooking, wines closed Thursdays and Sundays.
Parque Palmitos, 12 km north in the Barranco de Chamoriscán, tel. 928-760458, daily 9 am to 6 pm.
GOLF: Avda. Neckermann, tel. 928-762581, fax. 928-768245. 18-holes, driving range, restaurant.
GO-CARTS: Gran Karting Club, Tarajalillo (Maspalomas), Carretera General del Sur, Km 46, tel. 928-760090. The longest go-cart track in Europe, daily 10 am to 9 pm (winter), 11 am to 10 pm (summer).
AMUSEMENT PARKS: Holiday World, Campo Internacional, Lote 18, tel. 928-767176. Ferris wheel, shows, sideshows, daily from 6 pm; **Aqua Sur**, Carretera los Palmitos, Km 3, tel. 928-141905. Waterpark with slides, wave pool, daily from 10 am; **Parque Aquático**, highway exit 47, tel. 928-764361. Waterpark, wave pool, water slides, daily from 10 am.
Red Cross: In Maspalomas, tel. 982-762222; in Arguineguin, tel. 928-735911; **Police**: Tel. 928-141571; **Emergency**: Tel. 062.
POST OFFICE: Avenida de Tirajana 37.

Gran Canaria

PLAYA DEL INGLÉS

🛏 😊😊 **Hotel Eugenia Victoria**, Avda. de Gran Canaria 26, tel. 928-762500, fax. 928-762260. Oldish building, centrally located, inexpensive; **Sandy Beach**, Avda. Alfereces Provisionales, tel. 928-772726, fax. 928-767252. Near the beach, children welcome, group activities, tennis.

😊 **Apartamentos Royal Playa**, Avda. Alfereces Provisionales, tel. 928-760450. Near the beach.

❌ **Restaurante Tenderete II**, Avda. Tirajana, Edificio Aloe, tel. 928-761460. Small but excellent, vegetables from the garden, fish, kid.

🎠 **Mundo Aborigen**, culture park, Carretera Playa Inglés – Fataga (after 6 km), tel. 928-172295; daily 9 am to 6 pm, free bus.

🚵 *MOUNTAIN-BIKING:* **Happy Biking**, Centro Yumbo, tel. 928-768298. Bicycles and rollerblades for rent, tours organized, Mon-Sat 9:30 am to 1 pm and 6 to 9 pm.

DIVING: **Gran Canaria Diving Club**, Apart. Iguazu, tel./fax. 928-774539, courses, dives, daily 9 am to 8 pm.

🍸 *DISCOS:* Near the *Kasbah* shopping center **Joy**, **Pacha** and **Garage** (from 11 pm till dawn).

🎪 **Tienda de Artesanía del Cabildo Insular**, Avda. de España/corner Avda. de los Estados Unidos, crafts, Mon-Fri 10 am to 2 pm and 4 to 7 pm.

🚌 *BUS:* **Salcai**, Centro Yumbo, tel. 928-765332.

ℹ **Centro Insular de Turismo**, Avda. de España/ corner Avda. de los Estados Unidos, tel. 928-767848, fax. 928-771050; Mon-Fri 10 am to 2 pm and 4 to 7 pm, Sat 10 am to 1 pm.

PLAYA DEL TAURO

🛏 **Camping Guantánamo**, between Puerto Rico and Puerto de Mogán, tel. 928-560207. A square enclosed by a concrete wall, right next to the road, has sanitary facilities.

PUERTO DE MOGÁN

🛏 😊😊 **Hotel Club de Mar**, at the yacht harbor, tel. 928-565066, fax. 928-565438. Comfortable, with pool.

😊 **Pensión Salvador**, Calle de la Corriente 13, tel. 928-565374. Simple and clean.

❌ **Bodeguilla Juanana**, Local 390, tel. 928-565579. Popular restaurant at the harbor with good Canarian cooking and good wines; **Seemuschel**, at the harbor, tel. 928-565486. fish for gourmets, daily from 7 pm, closed in July and August.

🚤 *BOAT TRIPS:* Excursions in a submarine, from the harbor, tel. 928-565108.

➕ **First Aid**: Tel. 928-569222; **European Clinic Mogán**: Tel. 928-565090; **Emergency**: Tel. 062.

🚕 *TAXI:* Tel. 928-735000.

AIRPORT TRANSFER: Tel. 928-574141.

SAN AGUSTÍN

🛏 😊😊😊 **Hotel Gloria Palace**, Calle Las Margaritas, tel. 928-768300, fax. 928-767929. Modern establishment, beach access by road or footbridge; **Hotel Meliá Tamarindos Sol**, Calle Las Retamas 3, tel. 928-774090, fax. 928-774091. By the beach, with swimming pool.

😊😊 **Hotel Costa Canaria**, Calle Las Retamas 1, tel. 928-760220, fax. 928-761426, pool, park, near the beach.

❌ **Restaurante Buganvilla**, Calle Los Jazmines 17, tel. 928-760316. International cuisine, specialty is grilled perch (*cherne a la brasa*), dinners only.

🎠 **Sioux City**, Cañon del Águila, tel. 928-762573, 928-762982, Tue-Sun 10 am to 5 pm.

🍸 **Casino** in the Hotel Meliá Tamarindos Sol, tel. 928-762724. Dinner show, French restaurant, admission fee, daily 9 pm to 4 or 5 am.

🚤 **Nautico** diving school, tel. 928-770200, fax. 928-141805. From beginner to advanced.

➕ **Red Cross**: Tel. 982-762222; **Emergency**: Tel. 062.

🚕 *TAXI:* Tel. 928-763688.

AGAETE

🛏 😊😊 **Apartamentos El Angosto**, Paseo del Obispo Pildaín 11, tel. 928-554194.

❌ **Bar-Restaurante El Dedo de Dio**, Puerto de las Nieves, near Agaete, tel. 928-898000. Moderate prices, fish. View of the "Finger of God" rock formation, daily 10 am to 11 pm. Also organizes apartments.

🚤 **Reptilandia Park**, tel. 928-551269, turn off from the Agaete – Gáldar road, daily 11 am to 5:30 pm.

🚕 *TAXI:* Tel. 928-898020.

LOS BERRAZALES

🛏 😊😊 **Hotel Princesa Guayarmina**, at the end of the Valle de Agaete, tel. 928-898009, fax. 928-898525. Spa hotel with old-fashioned charm, garden, pool, restaurant. Dogs allowed.

PINAR DE TAMADABA

🛏 **Camping Tamadaba**, Magnificently situated campsite in the northwest of the nature reserve, only a water connection, but free of charge.

SAN NICOLÁS DE TOLENTINO

🛏 😊 **Hotel Los Cascajos**, Calle de los Cascajos 9, tel. 928-891165. Simple bed and breakfast.

➕ **Red Cross**: Tel. 928-892222.

🚕 *TAXI:* Tel. 928-898020.

THE NORTH

ARUCAS

❌ **Restaurante El Mesón de la Montaña de Arucas**, on Arucas' local mountain, tel. 928-601475. Canarian and international cuisine, good desserts.
➕ **Red Cross**: Tel. 928-601838.
🚖 *TAXI:* Tel. 928-600095.

FONTANALES

🛏 😊😊 **Hotel Rural El Cortijo**, Camino de Hoyas del Cavadero 11 (2 km outside, in direction of Pinos de Gáldar), tel. 928-610285. Country hotel 1,080 meters up, ideal for hikers and families. 7 double rooms, pool, restaurant, good Canarian cuisine, tel. 928-610283.

GÁLDAR

🏛 **Casa-Museo Antonio Padrón**, Calle Drago, tel. 928-551858, Mon-Fri 8 am to 2 pm, admission free.
➕ **Red Cross**: Tel. 928-552004.
🚖 *TAXI:* Tel. 928-881059.

GUÍA

🧀 *CHEESE:* **Queso de Guía** is available from two stores – at Marqués del Muni 34 (tel. 928-881875) and on the Carretera General, near the gas station.
➕ **Red Cross**: Tel. 928-882222.
🚖 *TAXI:* Tel. 928-882846.

MOYA

🏛 **Casa-Museo Tomás Morales**, Plaza de Tomás Morales, tel. 928-620217, Mon-Fri 9 am to 2 pm, free.
➕ **Red Cross**: Tel. 928-610222.
🚖 *TAXI:* Tel. 928-620083.

PUERTO SARDINA

❌ **La Fragata**, on the harbor mole, tel. 928-883296, fish, seafood, very good quality, high prices, Tue-Sun 11 am to 11 pm; **Bar-Restaurante Vistamar**, above the beach, inexpensive, seafood, daily noon to 11 pm.

TEROR

❌ **Bar-Restaurante Balcón de Zamora**, tel. 928-618042. Dining room has a view of Teror, large delicious helpings, simple Canarian food, moderate prices, Sat-Thu 8 am to 11 pm.
🏛 **Casa-Museo Patrones de la Virgen del Pino**, Plaza Nuestra Señora del Pino 3, Mon-Sat 11 am to 6 pm, Sun 11 am to 2 pm; **Studio** of the artist Georg Hedrich, in the house on the corner opposite the cathedral, tel. 928-631716. Visits Tue-Thu 11 am to 5 pm.
➕ **Red Cross**: Tel. 928-630190.
🚖 *TAXI:* Tel. 928-630289.

LAS PALMAS DE GRAN CANARIA

🛏 😊😊😊 **Hotel Reina Isabel**, Calle Alfredo L. Jones 40, tel. 928-260100, fax. 928-274558. On Canteras beach, two excellent restaurants, pool on the rooftop terrace, fitness center, comfortable rooms; **Hotel Santa Catalina**, Calle León y Castillo 227, Parque Doramas, Ciudad Jardín, tel. 928-243040, fax. 928-242764. Built in the neo-Canarian style, with a casino.
😊😊 **Hotel Los Bardinos**, Calle Eduardo Benot 3, tel. 928-266100, fax. 928-229139. Hotel tower in the Canteras quarter. Functional, balconies with sea view.
😊 **Hotel Madrid**, Plaza de Cairasco 2, tel. 928-360664. Built in the colonial style, located in Old Town.
❌ **Restaurante La Casita**, Calle León y Castillo 227, tel. 928-243831. Delicious food, closed Sun; **El Novillo Precoz**, Calle Portugal 9, tel. 928-221659. Grilled specialties, Tue-Thu 1 to 4 pm and 8 pm to midnight; **Bodegon Biberon**, Las Canteras, Pedro del Castillo 15, good pub, daily noon to 4:30 pm and 7:30 pm to 2:30 am; **Café del Real**, Calle Doctor Chil 19, tel. 928-318299. Café with tapas, Mon-Sat 7:30 am to 10 pm; **Terraza A Bordo**, Parque Alonso Quesada, open-air bar, July-Dec daily noon to 4:30 am; **Bar-Restaurant Off Shore**, Alonso de Ojeda, tel. 928-461555. At north end of Canteras Beach, American-style, families meet here during the day and young people at night, daily 11 to 2 am, Fri and Sat 11 to 4 am; **Terraza Horizonte**, Plaza de los Escritores (at Parque de San Telmo), open-air bar, Mon-Thu 11 to 2 am, Fri-Sun 11 to 4 am.
🏛 **Museo Canario**, Calle Doctor Chil 25, tel. 928-315600, Mon-Fri 10 am to 5 pm, Sat 10 am to 1 pm, Sun 10 am to 2 pm; **Casa-Museo de Colón**, Calle Colón 1, tel. 928-312373, Mon-Fri 9 am to 6 pm, Sat and Sun 9 am to 3 pm; **Centro Atlántico de Arte Moderno** (CAAM), Calle Los Balcones, tel. 928-311824, Tue-Sat 10 am to 9 pm, Sun 10 am to 2 pm; **Museo Pérez Galdós**, Calle Cano 6, tel. 928-366976; Mon-Fri 9 am to 1 pm and 4 to 8 pm; **Museo Diocesano de Arte Sacro**, Calle Espíritu Santo 20, tel. 928-314989, Mon-Fri 10 am to 5 pm, Sat 9 am to 2 pm; **Museo Néstor**, Pueblo Canario, tel. 928-245136, Tue-Fri 10 am to 1 pm and 4 to 8 pm, Sun 11 am to 2 pm.
🎭 **Teatro Pérez Galdós**, tel. 928-361509. Theater, dancing, music; **Centro Insular de Cultura**, Calle Pérez Galdós 5, tel. 928-371011. Exhibitions, readings, theater, film, Mon-Fri 11 am to 2 pm and 5 to 8 pm.
📖 **La Librería del Cabildo Insular de Gran Canaria**, Calle Cano 24, tel. 928-381539/594. Well-stocked bookstore, books about the archipelago; **Librería Archipiélago**, Calle Constantino 9, tel. 928-380006; **Tienda de Artesanía del Cabildo Insular**, Calle Domingo J. Navarro 7, tel. 928-369661, crafts, Mon-Fri

9:30 am to 1 pm and 4:30 to 8 pm, Sat 9:30 am to 1 pm; **Main Shopping Streets**: Calle Triana (pedestrian zone and Avda. de José Mesa y López with side streets. Bargains can also be found in the harbor district and at the **Flea Market**, on Sundays near the Mercado del Puerto.

➕ **Red Cross**: Tel. 928-222222.

🚌 *BUS*: City and southeast, **Salcai**, tel. 928-381110; city and northwest, **Utinsa**, tel. 928-360179.

TAXI: Tel. 928-462212.

BREAKDOWN SERVICE: Tel. 928-368761.

🛈 **Patronato de Turismo de Gran Canaria**, Calle León y Castillo 17, tel. 928-362222, fax. 928-362822; **Casa de Turismo**, Parque de Santa Catalina, tel. 928-264623, Mon-Fri 9 am to 1:30 pm and 5 to 7 pm.

THE EAST

AGÜIMES

🛏 **Turismo Rural de Agüimes S. L.**, tel. 928-124183, fax. 928-783663. The agency organizes renovated country houses in the medium to luxury categories.

❌ **Bar-Restaurante Tagoror**, end of the road in the Barranco de Guayadeque, tel. 928-172013, inside a cave, Canarian cuisine, daily 10 am to midnight.

➕ **Red Cross**: Tel. 928-182222.

🚌 *TAXI:* Tel. 928-180774.

ARINAGA

🏛 **Parque de Cocodrillo**, inland from Cruce de Arinaga, tel. 928-784725. Crocodile park, menagerie, feeding and shows, Sun-Fri 10 am to 6 pm.

INGENIO

🏛 **Museo de Piedras y Artesanía**, Mejías, Cam. Real de Gando, tel. 928-781124. North of Ingenio, stones, crafts, Mon-Sat 8 am to 6 pm, Sun 8 am to noon.

➕ **Red Cross**: Tel. 928-782222.

🚌 *TAXI:* Tel. 928-781585 and 928-782848.

TAFIRA ALTA / TAFIRA BAJA

🛏 **Hotel Golf Bandama**, near the Caldera de Bandama, tel. 928-353354. Small, with garden, next to the oldest golf course in Spain. Near Tafira Alta.

❌ **Restaurante La Masía de Canarias**, Calle Murillo 36, tel. 928-354040. Canarian cuisine.

🏛 **Jardín Botánico Canario Viera y Clavijo**, Tafira Baja, tel. 928-351645. Botanical garden with restaurant, Mon-Sun 9 am to 6 pm.

TELDE

🏛 **Casa-Museo León y Castillo**, Calle León y Castillo 43/5, tel. 928-691377, Mon-Fri 9 am to 2 pm; **Casas**

Consistoriales, old Town Hall, Pl. de San Juan 1, work by regional artists, Mon-Fri 8 am to 3 pm, 5 to 9 pm.

➕ **Red Cross**: Tel. 928-682222.

🚌 *BUS:* Tel. 928-690518.

TAXI: Tel. 928-694908.

SANTA BRÍGIDA

🛏 😊😊😊 **Hotel-Escuela Santa Brígida**, Monte Lentiscal, tel. 928-355511. Prospective hotel cooks can practice on guests here – the food is superb.

❌ **Restaurante Mano de Hierro**, Vuelta del Pino 25, tel. 928-640388. German cuisine with a Canarian touch, closed Sun, Mon evenings; **Restaurante Mallow**, Calle José Antonio, 5, tel. 928-641309. Traditional dishes, breakfast, tapas, daily 6 to 2 am.

🚌 *TAXI:* Tel. 928-640371.

THE CENTER OF THE ISLAND

CRUZ DE TEJEDA

❌ **Hostería Cruz de Tejeda**, tel. 928-666050. Parador restaurant, specialties include pumpkin soup, roast kid, almond cake, expensive, closed in the evening.

FATAGA

🛏 😊😊 **Hotel Rural Molina del Agua**, above Fataga, tel. 928-172089. Rooms, bungalows, pool, restaurant. Gofio mill, camel rides.

🐫 *CAMEL RIDES:* **Camel Safari Park La Baranda**, Fataga valley, tel./fax. 928-798680, daily 9 am to 6 pm.

SANTA LUCÍA

🛏 **Camping Temisas**, on the right of the road from Temisas towards Santa Lucía. Small, peaceful site, sanitary facilities are rudimentary.

❌ **Restaurante Hao**, main street, tel. 928-798007. Grill specialties, delicious Canarian cuisine, open daily until 6 pm.

🏛 **Museo del Castillo de Fortaleza**, on main street, tel. 928-798 007, Mon-Sat 8 am to 8 pm, Sun until 5 pm.

🚶 *HIKING* in small groups: Guido Miltenburg, El Papalillo 22, tel. 928-798693, fax. 928-798319.

VEGA DE SAN MATEO

🛏 **RETUR**: Vega de San Mateo, Calle Lourdes 2, tel. 928-661668, fax. 928-661560. Renovated country houses on offer, all categories.

🏛 **Museo Cho-Zacarias**, Carretera del Centro 22, tel. 928-660627, Mon-Sat 9:30 am to 1 pm. Has a good restaurant, Tue-Sun 1 to 4 pm, Sat, Sun reservations.

➕ **Red Cross**: Tel. 928-661049.

🚌 *TAXI:* Tel. 928-660345.

Gran Canaria

ADVENTURE HIKING

The island of Gran Canaria offers endless possibilities for hikers, ranging from a walk through the sand dunes to a rock-climbing tour. If your ambition were to cover all the hiking trails and paths of the island on foot, you would be hard pressed to cover the total of more than 300 kilometers of them. In the coastal regions you can hike to remote beaches and have a quiet picnic, at middle altitudes there are enticing expansive forests with several reservoirs that invite you to linger. In the heart of the mountainous region, enormous rock formations evoke feelings of great height, and in the fertile north you can hike through damp barrancos. Rock-climbing aficionados will find a real challenge in the vertical rock face of the Roque Nublo, among other climbs.

Previous pages: Fataga in the island's interior. Enjoying the scenery by mountain-bike. Above: Hiking in the region of Soriá. Right: At the Roque Nublo, the once sacred rock.

Hiking on Gran Canaria has a particular fascination: In contrast to the Alps, where the view from the summit may end at the next mountain range, you can look from the hills of the island almost to infinity over the broad expanse of the Atlantic. At the very least you will see the islands of Tenerife and La Gomera.

And yet you should not underestimate the hazards, even on this easy to explore island. Sudden changes in weather conditions or abrupt falls in temperature, often accompanied by quickly forming fog and sometimes gusty winds as well, are nothing unusual, particularly in the winter months. If you haven't got a good sense of direction, you might easily go astray, especially as there are hardly any designated trails here as there are in the Alps. On other days, the heat of the day might put you off your stride. If you think you can set off for your destination wearing only sandals, you could find yourself limping along with a sprained ankle. As a matter of principle, you should never undertake a hiking trip alone.

Tejeda – In the Heart of the Mountains

There are virtually ideal hiking conditions in Tejeda, which is centrally located in the mountains. It caters ideally to the needs of individualists by providing sufficient, inexpensive accommodation. If you stay here longer, you'll find plenty of trails to explore – and opportunities to escape from the crowds, too.

The awe-inspiring Roque Nublo rises above the scenery in mythic proportions. You will realize the significance that this enormous rock tower has on many inhabitants by having a look at the large number of photos and paintings in the local bar of the same name. Of course, every visitor wants to view the lord of the mountains from up close. To climb its 80-meter rock face demands a lot of skill, while the rocky plateau lying below is accessible to everybody. On a nice weekend this plateau resembles a pilgrimage site, as it can easily be climbed from the south. Starting from Tejeda, however, you can

link the Roque Nublo with a scenic and rewarding round-trip hike.

Follow the road from the center of Tejeda in the direction of Bartholomé. Once you have reached the Barranco de Tejeda, turn onto the hiking trail signposted "Trekking del Nublo." The path through the ravine, overgrown with bamboo and blackberry bushes, has recently been newly laid out, so that at present you can walk on a tarred road through La Culata further southwards. There are bars and shops here.

Carry on hiking uphill on the route marked with wooden signs through a beautiful pine forest. At the level of an abandoned cave dwelling, however, it is recommended to deviate from the main path and walk on a small path straight to the eastern face of the Roque Nublo until the path forks again.

Keep to the left and you will return to the main path. You climb up to the high plateau over a charming rock stairway. If you don't suffer from vertigo, take your time to clamber about the rocks a little,

59

from where you can catch some overwhelming views of the island.

When you descend, keep to the right at the first fork; half an hour later you'll reach a second fork. The path to the right leads straight back to La Culata, while the path to the left includes a rewarding detour through some rocky terrain up to the Degollada del Asserador crossroads. Here you can hike, completely on your own, through unspoiled and undeveloped nature, the path affording many stunning panoramic views.

Then you have to walk a few kilometers on a tarred road, unless you have arranged for a driver to pick you up. The road is not used much, however, and at the bottom of the first valley you can hike on the especially broad path, somewhat upwards, and reach a further observation point at the Cruz de Timagada. From here you can enjoy a magnificent view. Keep to the left at a junction just below the cross and climb down into the barranco where the signposted tour began.

Tejeda is also a good base to begin a walk to the Roque Bentayga, the cave site of Artenara, to explore the Tamadaba National Park on foot, or to take a detour to Cruz de Tejeda, located 500 meters higher up.

Hiking on Green Alpine Pastures

If you want to feel a touch of home, you'll do best by keeping to the north. Especially in winter and spring everything is turning green and bursting into flower as far as the eye can see. The bad news: It is often foggy, sometimes the sun does not come out at all. As compensation on cloudy days, you can watch the cows and sheep graze.

Rechts: The beach of Güigüí on the west coast is one of the island's most beautiful. The hike here from Tasártico will take you a good two hours.

The area around Teror is a classic example of lush pastures and a healthy growth of trees. During an excursion to the Finca de Osorio, where a number of celebrities would spend the night in times past, you roam, as the writer Miguel de Unamuno used to do, through prolific chestnut, oak and laurel woods. There is some cattle breeding here, too. On the occasion of the annual Fiesta del Pino, cows, bulls and calves are offered for sale at a livestock market. A round-trip walk through the park takes about an hour

In the Barranco de la Virgen, between Firgas and Moya, you get to know the damp north from its shadiest side. For one thing, bamboo, laurel and fern grow together to form a virtual thicket, for another, hardly any rays of light reach the narrow ravine. If you want to get into close contact with the dense botany of Gran Canaria, you can start along the "adventure gorge" (canyoning tours) from the coastal resort of San Andrés. You will cover an elevation gain of some 700 meters along this route. It takes a very good sense of direction, however, absolute surefootedness – and enough common sense to give up in case of heavy rainfall (at the halfway point the road between Firgas and Moya provides an opportunity to do so).

From Reservoir to Reservoir

In the south there are also excellent hiking areas, even if there is hardly anything to see apart from broom and gorse, and the landscape is perceptibly less hospitable. An outstanding hiking terrain, for instance, is the surroundings of Soría. From the reservoir of the same name, a very rewarding one-and-a-half-hour hiking-trip leads to the Embalse de Cueva de las Niñas.

Start out from the parking lot of the Casa Fernando restaurant, somewhat to the north of the village, and follow the road above the reservoir up to a palm

grove, in which a broad and clearly visible trail forks off. After a short while the route runs into a path, and you keep on walking straight towards a vertical rock face until you climb down to the bottom of the small barranco. In the spring you can hear the frogs croaking, while birds of prey find a retreat in the numerous natural caves all year round. Through richly varied vegetation you keep on climbing ever more steeply up to a mountain ridge, from which the view of the Roque Nublo gets better and better. Beyond the hill you cross a tarred road and climb down through the sparsely wooded forest, right to the basin of the reservoir. This is a first-rate picnic area.

For the hike back you can choose between either returning the way you came, or else making a broad detour on the way back to your starting point. For the latter option, keep to the northern bank of the reservoir and hike across country up to a finca hidden behind a hill. Take the narrow path that eventually joins the winding road back to Soría.

Detour to the Dream Beach

Many vacationers wanting to avoid the hustle and bustle of their hotel beach tend to look for a retreat at a quieter location, and they do not mind a lengthy march in order to find one. The Güigüi beaches, lying hidden on the west coast, are ideal for such an excursion. You start out from Tasártico, and walk a good four to five hours there and back.

You descend along a gravel road until a little path on your right branches off towards a telephone pole. The 550-meter Degollada de Aguas Sabinas pass, which has to be crossed, can be seen from afar. The real climb starts at the upper pass, but the gorgeous views of the sea and the cliffs make it worth the effort. What follows is the descent to the most beautiful beaches on the island, which only become visible shortly before you reach them. Be sure to bring enough water, because the finca selling drinks here is not always open. And don't underestimate the distance on your way back.

DEMANDING CYCLING TOURS

If a circular island with a diameter of just 50 kilometers has mountains up to 2,000 meters in height, it may give you a slight idea of what is in store for you: plenty of variations in altitude. Indeed, from all sides, steeply rising roads head up to the central mountainous region. You won't manage them too well unless you are an experienced and well-trained cyclist. There are hardly any leisurely flat stages along the way.

The well-trained cyclist, however, will be rewarded for his efforts, for this "miniature continent" offers an unprecedented diversity of landscapes in a very small space; moreso than any of the other Canary Islands. You can admire the breathtaking views into the valleys and the steep cliffs off the "dream route in the West," while in the center of Gran Canaria the much-cited "petrified storm" provides fascinating scenery surrounded by evergreen pine forests and reservoirs that offer great spots for a picnic.

There is a stunning contrast between the burnt soil of the sunny south and the flowering alpine meadows of the fertile north. The cyclist really gets to fully experience all of these contradictions here, with the wind wafting the rich scent of the forest and of the rugged mountains right under his nose.

Only those who have explored this variegated landscape both by car and by bike can know the true pleasure of cycling in unspoiled nature. And all along the way the islanders greet cyclists with warmth and hospitality.

As with everywhere in the Canary Islands, the authorities and tourism associations have not yet recognized the signs of the times and, despite the markedly growing demand for cycling paths, have

Right: The valley of Fataga has proven to be a popular and rewarding landscape for mountain-biking tours.

remained snoring away like Rip van Winkle while the rest of the tourism world passes them by. They keep on expanding freeways, landscaping new parks and constructing observation platforms with the help of EU funds – but cycling trails? A waste of time and money as far as most of them are concerned.

The individual traveler planning to explore the island by bicycle still meets with relatively unfavorable conditions. Only in Las Palmas and Maspalomas does one occasionally find a proper bicycle path. Still, the lack of signposting is much easier to live with than the insufficient number of accommodations that are willing to allow exhausted cyclists to stay for just a single night. On the other hand, in view of the mild nights during the summer season, spending the occasional night outside in your sleeping bag under the stars might even be preferable to sleeping in a rented room.

Rental Bike or Your Own?

Cycling enthusiasts have to consider before they begin their journey just how much they intend to indulge in their hobby. If you you are planning a number of lengthy tours during your holidays, it would probably be worthwhile bringing your own bike along to the island. Few people realize that most airlines will readily load your bike onto the plane, provided you have booked the transfer in advance, for an extra change of around US $25. You might be required at most to adjust the handlebars and let some air out of the tires.

For those using their trusty bicycle only sporadically, it is recommended that they avail themselves of local rental facilities; these are located above all in the south. But be aware of the quality on offer, make sure that the brakes, gears and saddle are properly adjusted. Most of all, take our advice and ask for a trial ride before actually renting the bike.

Happy Biking in Playa del Inglés offers good service and first-rate bikes, ranging from basic touring bikes up to the fully-sprung mountain bikes. Guided tours are available, as well. If you are interested, or if you'd like more information, contact Johannes Schöfecker at Happy Biking, Yumbo Center (lower level), Playa del Inglès, tel./fax 928-768298, mobile phone: 670-720505, e-mail: johannes @ideenet.com.

Day Trips to Get You Moving

There is an enormous range of possibilities for day trips on the island, with so many paved roads that touring and racing cyclists will surely be satisfied. Mountain bikers, on the other hand, will prefer cross-country routes.

It may be hard to imagine for sun worshipers in the south that, just a few kilometers away from the coast, trips on relatively calm roads through lush green valleys and narrow ravines into the interior are possible. It is nevertheless true.

From Playa del Inglés, as well as from Maspalomas, roads lead to the valley of Fataga, the Ayagaures reservoir and the Parque Ornitológico Palmitos. The trip each way for most tours is only around 30 kilometers; the route to the Palmitos Park is even somewhat shorter. The Palmitos Park provides an interesting destination, anyway. These routes are good for "warming up," too, especially in the evening when the landscape is bathed in pleasant, warm sunlight.

A much more demanding tour than this "warm up" is an excursion into the mountains, the climax being the round-trip tour to the well-known island rocks of Roque Nublo, Roque Bentayga and the Pico de las Nieves, at 1,949 meters the highest point on the island. This round trip, however, is hardly manageable within one day unless you have booked transport from Playa del Inglés to Ayacata, for instance with the Happy Biking fleet. Thus you start at an elevation of 1,290 meters, but you still have to manage difficult ascents. As you quite often have to strug-

63

Your next destination will be the Cruz de Tejeda. You'll reach it on a road that leads downhill for most of the trip.

At the Cruz, a stony wayside cross, you can watch the many tourists that have been given a lift up here by car or bus walking around with gooseflesh, because they often underestimate just how cool the weather is up here.

This pass is regarded as dividing the weather of the island and is quite often shrouded in mist, while just a few kilometers southwards the sun is steadily shining. The cyclist in a sweat will probably have to dress warmly here, too; for a fast descent to Tejeda, possibly the prettiest mountain village on Gran Canaria, is to follow.

After that you cycle onwards, straight towards the Roque Bentayga, and then climb up a further pass, the Degollada del Asserador. You can coast the remaining kilometers down to Ayacata.

Around the Island by Bike

Some sections of this high-altitude trip may easily be linked with a round-trip tour of the island. You can also cycle around the perimeter of the island, however, without heading for the central mountainous region. The following route is 200 kilometers long altogether, and may easily be managed within three or four days. This tour features breathtaking scenic contrasts as well.

Start by cycling leisurely from Maspalomas to Arguineguín using the coastal road 812. Here you have to consider how best to cover the 20 kilometers to Puerto de Mogán. The section to Puerto Rico, in particular, is much frequented in parts, so that you should try to avoid it if at all possible. Only if you start early will you have a good chance of avoiding the traffic jams. Otherwise, it would be an advantage to take the little ferryboat that leaves several times a day from Arguineguín.

gle against dense trade-wind clouds and cool winds, be sure to carry warm clothes with you.

At Ayacata you already find yourself surrounded by awe-inspiring mountains. From here, you can view weathered rock faces and enjoy the marvelous sights from one of the cafés, together with a well-deserved drink. It is recommended that you tackle the steepest section to the Roque Nublo first. Steep twisting roads lead to the symbol of the island and subsequently into increasingly dense pine forests. Here, shady barbecue spots invite you to linger awhile; drinking water is also available. Carry on to the wayside cross at the Cueva Grande and leave the peak of the Pico de las Nieves, which is "adorned" with a military base, to your right.

Above: The village of San Bartolomé de Tirajana in the island's interior. Right: The steep coast south of Agaete provides some of the best views to be found anywhere on Gran Canaria.

In Puerto de Mogán, you leave the coast and the crowds of tourists behind and head on a winding, slightly ascending road along the fertile Barranco de Mogán for the town of the same name. You can stop for a rest in the shadow of a mighty eucalyptus tree before the climb to the observation point of Degollado de la Alde starts in earnest. Here you can see vast tomato plantations with gigantic plastic sheets protecting the plants against wind and sun lying stretched out below in the valley. The steep descent quicky brings cyclists into the town.

Here you can pause once again for a short rest before tackling the second big stage of the trip, which starts above the small fishing port of Playa de la Aidea. You'll have to pedal up to an elevation of about 600 meters before you reach the rugged west coast. Here just about anybody would dismount from his or her bike in order to take in the amazing view of the nearly vertical cliffs.

The "dream road" now leads on to Agaete, and only gradually loses its charm. Unfortunately, you have to share the section to Gáldar with more traffic.

The green north can best be explored by taking the road to Moya from Santa María de Guía, and then heading for Teror via Firgas. This richly varied stretch leads through pine and laurel woods, densely overgrown barrancos and lovely secluded villages.

The town of Teror itself boasts a historic center and a number of colonial-style houses. From here you get to Telde, situated on the east coast, via Santa Brigída and Atalya.

Carry on cycling southwards via Ingenio to Aguimes, staying above the barren coast. Here you have two rewarding alternatives for the last ascent of your round-trip cycling tour: you can either make a wide detour on the 815 into the extensive Tirajana gorge, or go by way of the pretty mountain village of Temisas to Santa Lucía and San Bartholomé. After a pleasant descent through the valley of Fataga you eventually get back to your starting point.

Dreaming of Marlin

Sailing and sport-fishing belong to the top leisure activities of the island population. No wonder that numerous international trophies for deep-sea fishing in all of the world's oceans have been brought back to Gran Canaria. The most noticeable reason for these achievements is certainly the ideal training area, lying virtually on their doorstep in the clear waters of the Atlantic.

Fishing is possible in the waters off Gran Canaria throughout the year, however, in January and February some tours might take place on a limited scale only, owing to the rough sea. The hunt is then on for the various species of tuna, shark, barracuda, rays, dorado, wahoo, bonito, swordfish and sea perch. The catches vary according to the season: the best time for tuna (albacore, bluefin, yellowfin and bigeye) is between February and May, as well as in November and December. Wahoo is best caught in the months from July to October, while the best time of year for dorado is from May to September. Sharks, in contrast, may always be encountered off the coast. The much-sought-after blue and striped marlins may be caught successfully in summer and autumn, although you might have luck until well into December.

Vacationers may dream of the big catch in the harbor of Puerto Rico on the southwest coast of Gran Canaria. Everywhere where the boats land, photos of extremely happy anglers proudly presenting their catch are on display: they show gigantic marlins, enormous tuna, magnificent swordfish. Such trophies as these, however, will only be caught once or twice a year. Usually fishermen will have to be content with the smaller varieties they manage to reel in.

Anglers don't have any problems with the ownership of the catch, anyway, for the catch automatically belongs to the

Above: Who'll catch the biggest fish? Right: Enjoy the fishing, but not the fish – the catch belongs to the captain.

captain. Only smaller fish may sometimes be taken ashore by the fisherman, if he is lucky.

A deep-sea fishing tour, as a rule, takes about six hours. Most boats put off from the shore at the northen breakwater of Puerto Rico at about 9 o'clock in the morning, and get back at about 3 in the afternoon. Well-equipped boats have complete fishing equipment on board, including a flying bridge, fishing chairs, cabins, toilets and refrigerators, as well as an outrigger and a downrigger. For locating the fish and for optimal navigation, certain nautical equipment is required: a fish finder, a sonic depth finder, a sonar device for wreck fishing, an autopilot device, satellite navigation and radar devices. The personnel will readily advise you. If there is sufficient time, you can generally have a look at the boat before booking.

As a rule, the rates for a tour vary between about 5,500 and 7,000 pesetas. On some days so-called sunset tours are also offered; these are shorter and thus less expensive. Onlookers are usually also welcome on board and may join the tour at a reduced rate. Fishing gear and bait are provided by the boat hire company, so that you won't need to bring much along with you apart from a windbreaker and a lot of sun protection. Refreshments and a small snack are also normally included in the price.

In order to get a general idea of the usual catches as they come in, it is worthwhile watching the boats enter the harbor from about 2 o'clock in the afternoon onwards. There is no guarantee, however, that the same result will be achieved on the following day. In any event, it is recommended that you compare the rates of a number of companies before booking your fishing trip, and to book well in advance. Make sure that no more than three fishermen are going to be on one boat, because otherwise you are almost guaranteed to get in each other's way.

According to experience, the best time of year to be reasonably assured of a good catch is during the summer months, especially on those days when the sea is extremely calm. And while heading out to sea you should have the time to relax and take in the view of the impressive west coast of Gran Canaria dropping steeply into the sea.

The following boats offer excursions from Puerto Rico on a daily basis: the *Alcor III* and *Alcor IV*, telephone 928-735906; the *Barakuda dos* (catamaran), telephone 628-735080; the *Cavalier* and the *Dorado*, telephone 928-565521 (mobile phone: 689-692425); the *White Striker*, telephone 928-735013.

It doesn't always have to be deep-sea fishing, however; you may also reel in a few from the coast. There are some good fishing spots at the outer harbor wall of Puerto de Mogán and at the beaches of Playa de Veneguera and Playa del Asno. At both of these beaches you can even roast your catch over an open fire and enjoy the fish as fresh as they come.

Magnificent Diving

The abundance of fish species inhabiting the waters off the coast of Gran Canaria makes diving here an extra special experience. In the underwater world of the Canary Islands a large number of morays, globe fish, stingrays, groupers, breams, barracudas and cuttlefish may be observed. If you're especially lucky, you just might spot a dragonhead, a peacock wrasse, a stargazer or even an angel shark. Furthermore, on a nighttime dive you may get a chance to observe various types of shellfish leaving their hideaways in the rocks to go searching for food under the cover of darkness.

At the east coast the continuously rolling Atlantic waves have hewn very beautiful arches, chimneys, grottoes and caves out of the steep lava cliffs. The most beautiful diving areas of the island are lo-

Above: Preparing for an underwater adventure. Right: Divers can count on sightings of an unbelievable variety of tropical fish species.

cated on this coast, such as the underwater nature reserve of El Cabrón, near Arinaga, about 10 kilometers to the south of the airport. A myriad of fish species can be seen darting about between the lava rocks up to a diving depth of a good 30 meters. As the various points of entrance to the underwater nature reserve lie in particularly strong surf, however, even experienced divers should undertake their first dives on this island on the calmer southwest coast.

A special point of interest for divers is the wreck of a small cement freighter, the *Alexandra*, lying just 20 meters below the surface off Puerto de Mogán. It is within easy reach even for novice divers. This is also the best place for sightings of a somewhat unusual nature: the yellow submarine from Puerto de Mogán regularly passes the wreck on its sightseeing tour, about once an hour, so that passengers and divers get a chance to observe one another, as well as the fish.

The Dive Center Aquanauts, which has taken up quarters right beside the giant water slide at the beach of Puerto Rico, is ideally suited for beginners. The shallow basin off the beach, with its agreeable water temperature, makes learning the sport easy. Students pass a small footbridge and may comfortably climb straight into the sea water, which is just a few meters deep here. Here they can acquire a feeling for the sport of scuba diving.

The diving school, which is run by a group of Finns, offers a very relaxed atmosphere; students hardly ever find themselves under any stress. But Jarmo Råisänen, the head of the diving school, has something to offer to experienced divers as well. What he likes to do best is to take them out to the underwater national park of El Cabrón.

Generally speaking, rates for diving on Gran Canaria do not exceed the international average. There are various offers of guided dives, including equipment rental, ranging in price from about 6,000 to 6,500 pesetas. If you bring your own equipment, you pay 10 to 15 percent less. Diving courses, according to the standards of large international organizations such as CMAS or PADI, take four to five days and cost between 50,000 and 60,000 pesetas. Beginners are offered trial courses in the hotel swimming pool. Specifically for this purpose, the diving school personnel will come along with the required equipment, a real eye-catcher to sun worshipers lying in their deck-chairs. It is reasonable, however, to cast a somewhat critical eye over the diving schools when choosing the right one, for there are a few so-called "black sheep" on Gran Canaria, just as elsewhere, among them trying to make money with inadequate equipment and oversized diving groups.

If you do not want to start scuba diving right away, you can explore the underwater world by snorkeling just as well. Snorkeling equipment (mask, snorkel, flippers, wet suit) can be hired from any diving school for about 1,000 pesetas.

They will also advise you on where to find the best snorkeling spots. And another inside tip for night owls: Liliput, a small bar in Playa del Inglés – right beside the Kasbah on the first floor of the Centro Comercial Metro – is a great place to meet fellow divers. You might even find yourself a diving partner here.

The following diving schools conform to the international standards of PADI: Aquanauts Dive Center, right beside the giant water slide at the beach of Puerto Rico, telephone and fax 928-560655; Atlantic Diving, on the basement level of the Hotel Club de Mar in Puerto de Mogán, telephone 989-352049, fax 928-565438.

The following diving schools conform to the international standards of PDIC / IDA / CMAS: Diving Center Sun Sub, Hotel Buenaventure Playa, Plaza de Aniste, Playa del Inglés, telephone 928-778165, fax 928-773748; Diving Center Nautico, IFA Interclub Atlantic, Calle Los Jazmines 2, San Agustín, telephone 928-778168, fax 928-768122.

Greens beneath the Palms

The fantastic climate on Gran Canaria is absolutley ideal for golf, with hardly any restrictions due to the weather apart from the rather strong rays of the midday sun and maybe an occasional gust of wind. At present, afficionados can find two golf courses on the island: one of them is in the north near the capital Las Palmas, and the second is located in the middle of the holiday resort area in Maspalomas. Over the next few years, further courses are slated to be developed. The towns of Meloneras, El Sobre, Taurito and El Cortijo on the southwest coast, as well as Costa Botija in the north, are sites currently being discussed. How far these ambitious plans will be feasible, however, is still in question, for the lush greens may only be maintained by means of costly and lavish irrigation – and un-

Above: A great combination – a vacation in the sunshine and golf in Maspalomas. Right: About to tee off.

fortunately, cool water happens to be a rare commodity on Gran Canaria, as everybody knows.

The golf course of Maspalomas can be easily taken in from the vantage point of the small kiosk beside the tourist information office near Plaza Hierro. It is laid out between the palm grove on one side and the dunes of Maspalomas on the other. The access road via Avenida Touroperador Neckermann is signposted; in front of the grounds there is a large parking lot. Vacationers who are staying in the nearby apartment resort of Maspalomas can easily reach the golf course on foot.

Visitors will have to pay neither admission nor membership fees at the golf club of Maspalomas. If you want to play on the par-73 championship course, however, you will have to show proof of a minimum handicap of 34, if you are a woman, and of 27, if you are a man. Beginners who want to hone their skills can train with either of the golf pros who work at the club. The lessons cost 5,400 pesetas each. For those who haven't got their own equipment, golf clubs can be rented.

For one round on the 18-hole course adults are charged 9,500 pesetas; those under the age of 18 pay half price, i.e., 4,800 pesetas. If you pay for several rounds at once, you'll get a discount depending on the number of games: 12 rounds, for example, are 94,000 pesetas for adults. After 6 p.m. it is also possible to play a 9-hole round at about half-price. You may choose between holes 1 to 9 and holes 10 to 18.

The course is of medium difficulty, only a few of the many sand traps present a real problem. The tees are pleasantly arranged and some of the fairways are beautifully laid out between the Canarian Palms. The distances are not too long, nevertheless some players prefer to take an electric golf cart with them on their round. After finishing your game, you can have a drink or something to eat on the terrace of the club restaurant, which also provides a good opportunity to review the last round with your fellow players, and to arrange a date for your next game.

Address: Campo de Golf Maspalomas, Avenida Touroperador Neckermann, tel. 928-762581, fax 928-768245.

The second golf course on Gran Canaria is located at a distance of about 15 kilometers from Las Palmas, right beside the volcanic crater of Caldera de Baldama near Santa Brígida. The *Real Club de Golf de Las Palmas* (Royal Golf Club of Las Palmas) was founded by the British in 1891, and is thus the oldest in Spain. It is renowned for holding important international tournaments on a regular basis.

The course, which was designed by the famous Mackenzie Ross, conveys a very well-tended impression. Each individual fairway is entirely different and is quite demanding for players. The narrow and hilly course is a great challenge every time, even to professional golfers. Apart

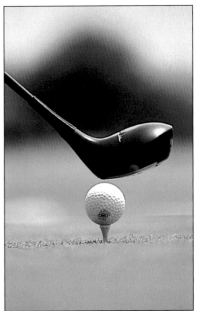

from that, there is an extensive training area that is, in part, illuminated by floodlights. Six golf pros are on hand for individual lessons.

Due to the great distance to the tourist resorts in the south of the island, however, this course may only be of interest to vacationers if they plan to stay in the adjacent golf hotel. Here they will also encounter a time-honored tradition of the British: at 5 p.m. tea is served in the hotel lobby among original British-style furnishings. This hotel may be booked through a travel agency; the golfing fee is included in the price of the room.

Addresses: Real Club de Golf de Las Palmas, tel. 928-351050.

Bandaura Golf and Country Hotel, tel. 928-353354, fax 928-351290. The hotel has 27 double rooms, a sauna, a heated swimming pool and a restaurant.

If you want to add to your golf equipment on Gran Canaria, you should be able to find everything you need at Abubilla Golf, Las Palmas, Calle Mesa de León, tel. 928-313459.

Surfboards in the Breeze

The trade winds blowing from the northeast that provide the region with its wonderful climate also blow to the great delight of numerous windsurfing enthusiasts. This is not the only reason, however, that the surfing spots on the southeast coast of Gran Canaria are considered among the best in Europe, for apart from the constant strong winds there are good waves which make the sport especially exciting hereabouts.

The advantages of Gran Canaria have also been discoverd by seven-time world champion Björn Dunkerbeck, who, together with his sister Brit, has opened a surfing center with a windsurfing school, equipment rentals and 25 bungalows. It is located on the Playa de Aguila in San Agustín. Here you can frequently observe both brother and sister playing with the

Above: Getting ready to brave the wind and the waves. Right: Experts especially are in their element here.

wind and waves, taking the full power of the wind in their sails with optimum control, and then lifting off to jump across the crest of a wave, or making use of the slightest motion of the waves when turning about in order to maintain their speed without the slightest loss of momentum.

In addition to the Dunkerbecks, the Club Mistral has established itself on Gran Canaria. Its center is located somewhat further to the northeast at the Playa de Tarajalillon, near the Aeroclub in Bahía Feliz. For this spot the probability of a wind force of four and more on the Beaufort scale is 60 percent between October and April.

In the summer months, when the wind on the east coast reaches a daily strength of seven to eight on the Beaufort scale, the beaches in Pozo Izquierdo and Vargas, which are usually rather deserted, come alive. In both places, which lie about five and ten kilometers respectively to the south of the international airport, crack surfers reach their top form in the enormous waves under before the eyes of the many spectators. If you want to participate, you have to have some experience with strong winds in order so safely cope with the thundering breakers. On the other hand, you are sure to receive appreciative looks in the Bar Los Bajas when the surfing community meets for a drink afterwards.

If you want to learn windsurfing on Gran Canaria, you will find numerous surfing schools on all the larger beaches from San Agustín and Playa del Inglés to Puerto de Mogán. Those places on the southwest coast which lie to the windward side of the northeastern trade winds offer excellent conditions for learning the ropes. Ideally suited is the harbor mole of Puerto Rico, where students are further protected against the waves. For a surfing course of several days you are normally charged about 21,000 pesetas; if you just want to rent a board you have to allow for around 2,000 pesetas an hour or 7,000 pesetas a day.

If you pay an extra charge, usually around US $50-75, most charter airlines allow you take your own board to Gran Canaria. This is only worthwhile in the case of a longer stay, though; unless you plan to spend every day windsurfing, it really isn't worth the hassle.

Playing with the wind and waves was a popular activity among youths from the coastal towns and fishing villages as much as a hundred years ago. They ventured out into the waves on their *panas* (small wooden boards) and let themselves be carried shorewards. Nowadays bodysurfing or surfing with a board, which preceded windsurfing, are still particularly popular among the natives. They splash about in dozens in the waves off the north coast, for instance at the beach of Las Canteras in the capital Las Palmas, as well as at the beaches of El Confital, San Andrés and Galdár. On the east coast, in the vicinity of Melenara, you may also watch the teenagers play their games with the waves. There are also suitable shops

with surfing equipment and board rentals on offer in the proximity of these beaches, of course.

Top addresses for windsurfers:

Surfcenter Dunkerbeck, Playa de Aguila, San Agustín, tel. 928-762958, fax 928-062989.

Surfclub Mistral, Playa de Tarajalillo, Bahía Feliz, phone and fax 928-157158.

Surfing and Sailing School Overschmidt, Gangway 1, in the harbor of Puerto Rico, tel. 928-182483.

Sailing repairs are carried out by Mario of the Hospital de Velas in virtually no time at all: Calle Santo Domingo 28, El Doctora, tel. 928-182483.

In the yacht harbors of Las Palmas, Puerto de Mogán, Puerto Rico, Pasito Blanco, Arguineguín and Agaete, numerous sailing schools have also been established. The offers range from beginners' and advanced courses up to participation in sailing regattas. For info contact the Federación de Vela Latina Canaria, Las Palmas, Esplanada Muelle Deportivo, tel. 928-293356.

Windsurfing

CANARIAN CUISINE
Substantial and Delicious

The Canary Islands have been one of the most popular vacation destinations with Europeans for decades now, so it's no surprise to encounter dishes from all the tourists' countries of origin when you go out to eat in the large resorts here. With all the Irish pubs and Bierkellers everywhere, it's hard to find anything authentically Canarian.

If you really want to get to know Canarian cuisine, you'll need to head inland. Restaurants can be divided into three categories: simple, small ones with good home cooking; large excursion places with meat and seafood specialties, where local families take all their relations at weekends; and rather expensive

Above: Mojo, a dip that comes in a number of variations, gofio and watercress soup are all important components of Canarian cooking. Right: Dried fish is often offered for sale right in the harbor.

gourmet establishments where refined Canarian cuisine is served to those able to afford it.

Canarian cuisine originated as the rural cooking of the Spanish and Portuguese immigrants, enriched by influences from Latin America. The wealthier households enjoyed produce grown on their own estates, or imported from overseas. Very filling meat dishes and sweet desserts were a regular feature of every main meal, and still are today. In the coastal towns seafood, simply but deliciously prepared in a variety of ways, was the main dish. Day laborers and their wives often had to rely on *gofio* and potatoes as basic foodstuffs. *Gofio*, roast flour made of wheat, maize or chickpeas, is one of the few foods that still dates back to the times of the Guanches.

Each household had (and still has) its own recipe for the typical sauce known as *mojo*, of which there are four basic types: a spicy mojo, with small red chili peppers marinated in olive oil and wine vinegar (*mojo picón* or *mojo rojo*); a green mojo with herbs (*mojo verde*); a garlic-dip mojo (*mojo de ajo*); and finally a saffron mojo with oregano and garlic (*mojo de azafrán*).

Tapas, those delicious Spanish appetizers, are available in almost all the restaurants and bars on the islands. They can range from cheese with olives to ham, vegetables, fish and meat, all served in delicious sauces.

Thick Soups and Hearty Stews

A soup is often served before the main course. There are various kinds of fish soup, and also vegetable soups known as *potajes*, which are usually very thick because of their high potato content. Pumpkins, cabbages and beans are also popular ingredients. One popular soup of the day is *sopa de berros*, made from watercress. If you order a *sopa de garbanzos* (chickpea soup) you'd better be hungry, because it's often as filling as an entire meal.

Stews play a great role in Canary Island cookery. A *puchero canario* contains up to seven different kinds of meat, all cooked with tomatoes, carrots, onions and chickpeas. Together with that there's a broth composed of beans, white cabbage, yellow squash, sweet corn, sweet potatoes and taro root. To spice things up a bit the locals use crushed garlic cloves, pepper, cloves, oil, and – if you want a really filling meal – some salted meat and *chorizo,* a smoked red sausage. Sliced pears or other fruit may also be added.

First you eat meat and vegetables; then you take some *gofio* flour out of a bowl and roll it into balls before dipping it into whatever sauce you have left on your plate – it's a delicious and very filling side dish. Whatever sauce is left behind after the *gofio* is eaten with a spoon.

Other stews include *sancocho*, a simple vegetable stew which is usually livened up with meat or fish (usually dried fish), and *olla potrida*, which usually consists of beef, sausage and vegetables.

Marinated Rabbit

It's virtually the Canarian national dish: marinated rabbit with boiled potatoes (*conejo en salmorejo con papas arrugadas*). The rabbit is left to marinate in a mixture of garlic, parsley, oregano, thyme, paprika, salt, pepper, oil and vinegar for at least one night. Then it gets basted in a ceramic pot until the flesh almost falls from the bone, while being sprinkled at intervals with wine. Small, whole potatoes are served as a side dish, boiled in their skins in a pot of seawater, so they crinkle up and get a shiny white crust of sea salt.

Fresh Seafood

Delicious fresh fish is served in the fishing villages of all the Canary Islands, and in the best restaurants you can choose it for yourself. The range on offer usually includes hake (*merluza*), angler fish (*sama*), sole (*lenguado*), sea bass (*mero*) and a kind of brace (*vieja*). On top of that

they have tuna fish steaks (*atún*), sword-fish (*pez espada*) and also shark (*tibu-rón*). Try the brace baked in salt, too (*dorada a la sal*).

If you're not that hungry, and don't mind such things, there's octopus (*pulpo*) and squid (*calamares*), marinated as *tapas*. From depths of up to 700 meters they catch shrimps (*cangrejos*), prawns (*gambas*) and lobster, including the elon-gated *langostas canarias*. If you're unfa-miliar with dried cod (*bacalao*), only eat it if it's recommended.

Desserts

After the meal, before coffee and/or *coñac*, Canarios indulge in a sweet and usually high-calorie dessert (*postre*). The flambéed bananas are filling, as are *tur-rón de gofio*, an almond dessert made of honey, flour and figs, *bienmesabe*, a

Above: Tuna fish, fresh from the boat. Right: Checking the wine's color as a prelude to tast-ing it.

sweet dish made of eggs and almonds, and *frangollo*, which is made of maize and milk. Alternatively you can have a piece of fresh fruit.

Cheese

Smoked and unsmoked sheep and goat cheese is produced on all the islands; it usually tastes strong and slightly salty. The simple goat's cheese *queso blanco* is served almost everywhere. A local spe-cialty is the mild cheese known as "flower cheese" (*queso de flor*) from Gran Canaria, produced in Guía from fresh sheep and cow's milk. This flower cheese – which gets its name from the bluish-purple artichoke flowers used in its production – comes in three stages of ripeness: *tierno* (soft/young), *semiduro* (half ripe) and *viejo* (old), and is very de-licious indeed. Incidentally, there's usu-ally a very broad assortment of cheeses on sale at any of the markets, and you can also ask the farmers themselves what kind they produce.

Drink

The mineral water (*agua mineral*) on the islands is good, and can be ordered either *con gas* or *sin gas* (carbonated or non-carbonated). The fruit juices (*zumos de fruta*) are usually freshly squeezed, and the milkshakes (*batidos*) are often mixed with ice cream or fruit. A particularly creamy and interesting one is the light-green *batido de aguacate*, which is made from avocados.

For warmer temperatures, assuming it's drunk in moderation, the local beer (*cerveza*) is ideal; it comes in two brands, "Dorada" and "Tropical." At mealtimes, wines from Lanzarote and Tenerife are recommended; good-quality Spanish mainland wines are also available. There's a choice between *vino tinto* (red), *rosado* (rosé) and *blanco* (white). The quality of a Rioja is often better than that of a local Canarian wine, but sometimes there are some delicious surprises. The whites from Lanzarote have a very special flavor, deriving from the volcanic soil. To go with coffee afterwards, instead of a dessert wine you can also try *ron miel*, a honey rum, or a banana liqueur (*crema de banana*). Restaurants attached to wine estates often serve *Aguardiente de Parra*, a clear spirit distilled on the premises.

If you feel like coffee after the meal, you can have a *café solo*, an ordinary small black espresso, or a *café doble* which is the same thing only twice as big. If there's a little milk inside, it becomes a *café cortado*, which is far more popular with the locals than regular coffee with milk (*café con leche*). German-style filter coffee is also available in some places as *café alemán*.

In the tourist centers, exotic cocktails are ubiquitous. All the known types, from Planter's Punches to Singapore Slings – get brought to tables with sparklers attached to them. One simpler and yet equally good cocktail is a *Mojito Cubano*, a mixture of Havana rum and fresh mint which was brought back here from Cuba by returning emigrants.

ARTS AND CRAFTS
OF THE CANARY ISLANDS

The steady increase in visitors to the Canary Islands has also resulted in an expanding market for souvenirs, especially typical arts and crafts products made on the islands. Professions that were threatened with extinction during the industrial age have been given a new lease of life by tourism, and are often state-subsidized into the bargain.

Roseta

Vilaflor or Tenerife lace, very time-consuming to make and very beautiful, was an export article as long ago as the 19th century. *Roseta* is the name given to it because the basic form is a rosette, although there are numerous variations, including stylized fish, butterflies or flowers. Several of the rosettes can be joined together to make a tablecloth, and the women often work for years on end to create valuable cloaks and mantillas. Despite competition from China, which mass-produces the same thing, Rosetas on Tenerife are still made by hand: in Vilaflor, La Escalona, Arona, Valle de San Lorenzo, San Miguel and Granadilla. The preferred color for the lacework is white or a natural color, though black is always the color chosen for a mantilla. On Lanzarote (in San Bartolomé, Teguise and Tinajo) the women usually produce their rosetas in blue, green and yellow.

Calados

Traditional hem-stitch embroidery (*Calados*) involves removing a number of strands from a cloth and then turning the fronds into attractive and subtle patterns which are usually geometrical. Calados centers on Tenerife are all located along

Right: An age-old trade that is still important today – a basket-maker shows his skill.

the north coast, from Victoria de Acentejo as far as Buenavista. In Orotava young women are trained in the art at the Casas de los Balcones, so the tradition doesn't die out. A common pattern in the south of Tenerife, in the villages of Fasnia, Granadilla, Chimiche and El Escobonal, is a spidery one known as *arañón*. The bastions of calados on Gran Canaria are Gáldar and Moya in the north, and Ingenio, Agüimes and San Bartolomé de Tirajana in the south. Traditional centers on Fuerteventura, alongside the capital, are Lajares, La Oliva, Tindaya, La Mantilla and Tetir in the north, and Betancuria, Triquivijate, Antigua, Los Llanos and Casillas del Ángel in the center.

Silk

El Paso on La Palma was once a silk production center with its own silkworm farm and numerous mulberry trees. All that remains today is a small factory that makes ties, scarves and handkerchiefs, and it is run by Doña Bertila Pérez González. All the silkworms come from Japan, and live in shoeboxes full of mulberry leaves. Señora Bertila, who has received several awards for her services to the silk industry, can explain each phase of the process to you. She colors her material with natural dyes.

Basketry and Weaving

Wherever the Canary Islands have preserved their original, rural character, basket weaving still plays a role; straw, reeds and palm leaves are all used as materials. The latter are used to make artistic decorations frequently encountered at church festivals, e.g., Palm Sunday. The finely-woven straw hats from Yaiza and Tinajo on Lanzarote are also an exquisite rarity, and are correspondingly difficult (and expensive) to get hold of. They make a perfect souvenir, however.

Pottery

The Guanches modeled their ceramic products without the use of a wheel, and this technique is still used in many places on the Canary Islands. There may not be any direct connection with the Guanches in this regard at all, in fact, but instead with immigrants who came here from Galicia, where pots were also made using this technique. In Victoria de Acentejo on Tenerife, some families still make ceramic vessels in the traditional manner; pottery is also produced in the museum of Arguayo, and in Santa Cruz de Tenerife there's an employment program called "Potting without a Wheel" (Centro Ocupacional San José Obrero, Calle Marisol Marín 5).

The pottery centers on Gran Canaria can be found at La Atalaya and Hoya de Pineda. Here, as well as in Santa Lucía de Tirajana, clay copies of ancient Guanche figures are also manufactured. The equivalent location on the island of La Palma is at Hoyo de Mazo, where potters can also be seen working away. On La Gomera, the most important ceramic production center is Chipude.

Cigars and Timples

Some craft centers, such as the Patio Limonero in Garachico on Tenerife, allow visitors to watch cigars being made by hand. There's also a modest homemade cigar business run by several old men in El Paso. Canarian cigars taste good, and if you're a smoker, or know any, they make excellent souvenirs.

A typically Canarian folk instrument is the *timple*, a kind of small guitar with a rounded soundboard, resembling a mandolin. The most famous timple factories in the Canary Islands can be found in Teguise (Lanzarote). Musical instruments such as guitars, chácaras and also tambourines are manufactured in La Orotava, Playa de San Juan (Tenerife), Taibique, Sabinosa, Guarazoca (El Hierro), Hermigua (La Gomera) and Telde (Gran Canaria).

FLORA AND FAUNA

The flora of the Canary Islands is utterly fascinating. It's not only the sheer variety of plants here that is so astonishing, but their size as well. The tiny poinsettia familiar from flowerpots in Europe grows to the size of a small tree here on the islands.

There are around 3,000 different plant species on the Canaries. Many were introduced as useful plants or as ornamentals, while some traveled here as "stowaways" on board ships and went to seed. What makes the flora of the Canaries so exotic is not only the imported tropical plants but also the very high proportion of endemic varieties. Around 585 different plants are native to the islands, whereby around 370 species are endemic – i.e., they occur on just one island, and sometimes even in just one barranco.

Above: Aeonium holochrysum, an endemic, thick-leaved plant. Right: North African ground squirrel. Following pages: Canarian folklore.

The highest proportion of wild plants can be found on Tenerife and Gran Canaria, with 1,300 and 1,260 different species respectively; the lowest is Hierro, with 530 species. Tenerife occupies a special place among the islands in that its climatic zones enable a very large number of different plants to grow. It has 135 endemic species which have now been transferred to the neighboring islands. In this way, Tenerife has 21 of the same species as Gran Canaria, 65 kilometers away. Some of these endemic plants, including the legendary dragon tree, the Canarian laurel and several Canary ferns originate from the Tertiary Period, and can only be found in fossilized form in more northerly regions.

Dragon Trees and Euphorbias

The botanical symbol of the islands is the dragon tree (Spanish: *drago*), which was worshiped as a sacred tree back in the Guanche era. It isn't a tree at all actually, but a member of the lily family, and since it has no rings, guessing its age is not easy. When the bark is scratched it emits a colorless sap which goes dark red on exposure to the air. This liquid was used medicinally by the Guanches, and they also embalmed the bodies of their dead with it.

If you hike through the dry zones you'll encounter the endemic Candelabra euphorbia (Spanish: *cardón*), which, like all euphorbias, excretes a milky acidic juice. This also applies to its rather similar relative the King Juba euphorbia (*tabaiba*), recognizable by its reddish fruit capsules above a wreath of pointed leaves. It is believed that the Guanches used juice from this plant to anesthetize fish before catching them.

The Canary palm, which resembles a date palm, is extremely elegant. Its fruit is only eaten by birds and rats, and street-cleaners use its leaves as brooms. The Canary pine is important for the islands' water supply. It has needles up to 30 cen-

timeters in length which "comb" the fog up in the mountains, thereby providing the soil with moisture. It has also proven extremely resistant to forest fires.

The most unusual flower on the islands is the red Teide echium, which grows in the Cañadas at the foot of Mount Teide and blooms from May to early July. It grows as high as a man, and one plant can produce up to 84,000 red blossoms. Also known as "The Pride of Tenerife," it has now been successfully planted on Gran Canaria.

Few other plants manage to survive in the desert-like, arid landscape above the tree level, but one which does is *retama*, the pink-and-white Teide broom (*Spartocytisus nubigens*).

The author Miguel de Unamuno regarded the thorny lettuce (Spanish: *ahulaga*), though not endemic, as best embodying his vision of Fuerteventura as a dried-out, skeleton-like island. Adapted to suit a desert-like climate, this plant has reduced its leaves to the bare minimum: they have become thorns.

Lizards and Canaries

The Canary Islands only have a modest amount of wildlife. Domestic pets excepted, there are no large mammals apart from moufflons, a species of shaggy sheep imported several years ago. Their population has swelled since then, and because they threaten the flora on Mount Teide they are being hunted to keep their numbers down. Rabbits live wild, but usually land up on menus. More unusual fauna includes certain (harmless) reptiles, and also the giant lizard. The gecko (Spanish: *perenquén*) is a common sight in houses, and eats insects. There are several Canary lizards, one species of which lives on Hierro and grows to a length of 60 centimeters. Other native animals include the Canary skink.

The most famous bird, of course, is the canary. The wild ones don't sing at all, by the way; only when they're caged and taught to do so. Their plumage is also a subdued grayish-green, rather than dazzling yellow.

81

METRIC CONVERSION

Metric Unit	US Equivalent
Meter (m)	39.37 in.
Kilometer (km)	0.6241 mi.
Square Meter (sq m)	10.76 sq. ft.
Hectare (ha)	2.471 acres
Square Kilometer (sq km)	0.386 sq. mi.
Kilogram (kg)	2.2 lbs.
Liter (l)	1.05 qt.

TRAVEL PREPARATIONS

Tourist Information

In the UK: Spanish Tourist Office, 57-58 St. James's Street, London SW1A 1LD, tel. (0171) 499-0901. For brochures, tel. (0891) 669920.

In the US: Tourist Office of Spain, 665 Fifth Avenue, New York, NY 10022, tel. (212) 759-8822; 8383 Wiltshire Boulevard, Suite 960, Beverly Hills, CA 90211, tel. (213) 658-7188; Water Tower Place, Suite 915 East, 845 North Michigan Avenue, Chicago, IL 60611, tel. (312) 642-1992, 944-0216, fax. (312) 642-9817; 1221 Brickell Avenue, Miami, FL 33131, tel. (305) 358-1992, fax. (305) 358-8223.

In Canada: 102 Bloor Street West, 14th Floor, Toronto, Ontario M5S 1M8, tel. (416) 961-3131, 961-4079, fax. (416) 961-1992.

In Australia: 203 Castlereagh Street, Level 2, Suite 21a, PO Box 675, 2000 Sydney, NSW, tel. (02) 264-7966.

Internet Addresses

The following Internet addresses can be very useful sources of additional information before traveling to Gran Canaria:
Canary Islands: www.members.aol.com/canconsult/links.htm.
Gran Canaria: www.idecnet.com/patronatogc.

Spanish Embassies

UK: Spanish Embassy, 20 Peel Street, London W8 7PD, tel. (0171) 727-2462, 243-8535, fax. (0171) 229-4965.

US: Consulate General of Spain in New York, 150 East 58th Street, New York, NY 10155, tel. (212) 355-4080, fax. (212) 644-3751.

Canada: 74 Stanley Avenue, Ottawa, Ontario, Canada K1M 1P4, tel. (613) 747-2252, fax. (613) 744-1224.

Entry Regulations

If planning to stay for up to three months, visitors need to have a valid passport. Anyone planning to stay longer than that needs to get a visa from the Spanish embassy or consulate in his or her native country.

Visa extensions while on the Canaries have to be applied for at the *Gobierno Civil* in Santa Cruz de Tenerife or Las Palmas de Gran Canaria. An application certification from the consulate of one's own country is needed for this, along with an application certificate for the municipality in which one intends to reside. In addition, one must show proof of having health insurance. In certain cases an adequate income has to be proven by bank guarantee.

Anyone arriving by ferry in their own car needs the green international insurance card, as well as the usual papers and driver's license.

For pets, such as cats and dogs, an official veterinary certificate is required to be shown which may not be older than two weeks and must confirm in both English and Spanish that the animal has been vaccinated against rabies within the past year, and at least one month before entry.

Health

The same guidelines apply for the Canary Islands as for Europe. Vaccinations against tetanus and polio might be considered. There are good pharmacies almost everywhere on the islands.

Many common medications are available from the pharmacies on the island, even though they may have different names here. If you bring along the paper normally enclosed with medications, or a at least a description of the medication from your physician, the Spanish pharmacist can generally work out what you need from that and provide you with the Spanish equivalent.

Under EU regulations, an E111 form should provide treatment for residents of Great Britain while on Gran Canaria. This can often lead to delays and red tape, however, so it's best to have your own private insurance if possible. American visitors should also check that their health insurance gives them adequate coverage, and take out an additional travel insurance policy if necessary.

The standard of health care in the hospitals here is first class, and many towns also have a facility that can provide first aid or emergency treatment. Most doctors speak good English.

Ambulances will take you to the nearest hospital that is available, which will treat your complaint, but many are private and will only treat you if you have private medical insurance – so it's very important to have the relevant documents.

Pharmacies can be recognized by the green or red Maltese crosses on the sign outside, and in the cities and larger towns there is always at least one emergency pharmacy open all night long (see also "Medical Treatment / Pharmacies," on page 89).

Clothing

For a pure beach holiday you'll be fine with just light summer clothing in both summer and winter; warmer clothing is only needed in the evenings, or if a wind blows up. Despite the mild temperatures on Gran Canaria, you should not underestimate the power of the sun – good sun protection is essential, especially if the weather is windy.

Even though casual clothing is usually okay, the better hotels on the islands consider etiquette important at mealtimes, and especially in the evenings, when more formal clothing is required; the same applies to expensive restaurants and cultural events.

Those who have chosen accommodation at higher altitudes (from 500 meters to over 1,500 meters), or are planning on hikes in the mountains, must expect repeated rain showers and cooler temperatures (up to 10°C cooler than on the coast). Bring along rain protection, a light sweater or jacket, and sturdy shoes for unsurfaced paths.

When to Go

Gran Canaria is a popular travel destination all year round. The peak season is during European vacation times, in fall, at Christmas, carnival time and Easter, and flights and accommodation have to be booked well in advance, often up to six months before your trip. In winter a lot of old-age pensioners come here to stay warm, while in the summer you're more likely to meet young and middle-aged people.

Currency Exchange / Regulations

Until it gives way to the Euro, the Spanish peseta (abbreviated "Pta") is the country's unit of currency. There are 20,000, 10,000, 5,000, 2,000 and 1,000 Pta banknotes; 500, 200, 100, 50, 25, 10, 5, 2 and 1 Pta coins. The 5-Pta coin is known familiarly as a *duro*.

The current exchange rate is:
US $1 . . . . 174 Ptas
UK £1 . . . . 278 Ptas
AUS $1. . . . . 106 Ptas

Incidentally, a little sound financial advice: Only exchange a small amount of pesetas at home, enough to keep you until you can get to a bank, because the exchange rate on the island is usually a lot better. Any amount of foreign currency can be brought with you to Gran Canaria.

Guidelines

If you want to take out large sums of money, it's best to declare it – because the maximum permissible amount per person without declaration is up to one million pesetas and foreign currency with an equivalent value of 500,000 Ptas.

There are automatic cash dispensers at all the holiday resorts and large towns (on Hierro in Valverde and Frontera). Traveler's checks, cash and Eurochecks can be exchanged at any bank. Credit cards are accepted nearly everywhere – apart from Hierro, where they are the exception to the rule (see also "Banks," page 88).

ARRIVAL

By Plane

A lot of European charter flights go directly to the Canary Islands. Gran Canaria is also served by larger airlines, such as British Airways, Air France, Iberia, Lufthansa, Swissair, etc.

In general, package tours are cheaper than holidays tailored to one's own preferences – and so comparing prices and offers by various travel agents is always a good idea. Most charter flights allow 20 kilograms of luggage, though if you're planning to stay longer you can apply to have the amount increased.

Special luggage (such as sports equipment) has to be reported in good time; a bicycle or surfboard usually costs around US $50-75 extra. If you want to take your pets along too (in special containers), that has to be officially applied for as well. The price of the journey is based on the weight of the animal.

Passport checks are quite rare within the EU, which saves a lot of time and hassle, and luggage is only examined in special cases (suspected weapons or drugs, etc.). The procedure is a lot stricter for intercontinental flights.

In the arrivals hall you will find rental car companies, automatic cash dispensers, tourist information, a post office and a currency exchange outlet.

Just after arrival at the airport is a good time to exchange your currency for pesetas – you might be surprised at how favorable the rates are.

By Ship

From Cádiz (on mainland Spain) a ferry of the *Companía Trasmediterránea* arrives every Saturday, with stops in Las Palmas de Gran Canaria (the trip takes around 48 hours).

In the summer you have to book months in advance, mainly because of the relative lack of transportation capacity for automobiles.

Timetables, prices and applications can be obtained from **Companía Transmediterránea**, Plaza Manuel Gómez Moreno, E-28020 Madrid, tel. 91423-8500 or 91423-8832. Branch office: Avda. Ramón de Carranza 26/7, E-11006 Cádiz, tel. 95628-7850.

ISLAND-HOPPING

By Plane

Flights run by Iberia and its subsidiaries, or by other private firms, travel between the islands several times a day, and no flight takes longer than one hour. These flights can be booked at travel agencies at home, at the agencies in the Canary Islands themselves, from Iberia (also for its subsidiaries) or directly at the airports.

By Ship

The cheapest way of getting from Point A to Point B is to "island-hop" by ferry. All the islands are connected by car ferry, though not always directly. Some routes, such as those between Tenerife and Gran Canaria, Tenerife and Gomera, and also Gran Canaria and Fuerteventura, are served by jetfoils, but these are senstive to choppy seas and don't always run.

Competing for ferry traffic are the state-run *Companía Trasmediterránea* (Las Palmas de Gran Canaria, tel. 928-

260070; see p. 86), its subsidiary *Naviera Armas* (Las Palmas de Gran Canaria, tel. 928-474080) and the private shipping company *Líneas Fred Olsen* (Santa Cruz de Tenerife, tel. 922-628200). The price differences between all three are minimal. Tickets can be booked via travel agencies or at the companies' respective harbor offices. Tickets are usualy still available just before departures apart from on public holidays, so booking ahead isn't always a must.

GETTING AROUND ON GRAN CANARIA

By Bus

All the islands have efficient public bus service networks. On Gran Canaria two companies have split up the business for themselves, and you only ever see both of them at the same time in the capital. Larger towns are served several times a day, but small villages aren't always part of the network (see the *INFO* section on pages 50-53).

Timetables are available at larger bus terminals, near tourist offices, at the airports or in the vacation resorts. Group tickets and multiple-journey tickets can often be a lot cheaper than the usual rate (for example, the *Tarjeto Dinero* on Gran Canaria).

By Taxi

Taxicabs are relatively inexpensive, but it's always best to settle on a price with the driver before you start to move. For overland trips it's a good idea to ask for a look at the list of fixed tariffs. As a rule, one kilometer costs 100 pesetas, though short trips are a bit more expensive. There's also an official surcharge for trips on Sundays and public holidays.

By Rental Car

Rental cars in the economy car category cost a weekly rate of between 2,200 and 2,500 pesetas a day, plus insurance of around 1,200 pesetas a day. If you're staying longer you can generally negotiate a better rate.

The international car rental companies will organize your car for you before you leave on vacation, but it's also possible to take advantage of local competitiveness and negotiate a deal with the smaller companies on the islands themselves. If you do find a cheap offer, make sure the vehicle is roadworthy, and also check the size of the rental fleet – just so you don't have to waste two valuable days of your vacation waiting around for a substitute vehicle that never appears.

A national driver's license is sufficient for renting a car. There is often a clause in the contract that says the driver has to be at least 21 years old. If you want others to drive as well as you, their names have to be entered in the contract and their respective licenses shown, too.

Hitchhiking

On the island the locals hitchhike quite a lot, but that's usually because they know the drivers passing them. Tourists have a much harder time of thumbing a ride.

Traffic Regulations

Basically the traffic regulations are the same as the rest of Europe. Cars drive on the right, and seat-belts have to be fastened, even in town traffic. The alcohol limit is 0.8 – and police checks are particularly frequent late at night whenever there's a fiesta on. At traffic circles, unless otherwise indicated, the vehicle arriving from the right has priority.

If you suddenly have to slow down or stop because of an obstacle in the road, you can warn the driver behind by switching on your left indicator or sticking your left hand out of the window. On winding mountain roads it's always best to sound the horn before a bend.

In the Canary Islands the speed limit in built-up areas is 60 kph, on country roads 90 kph, on major roads 100 kph and on

Guidelines

highways 120 kph. On weekends some people tend to travel amazingly quickly, and enjoy overtaking on bends, but most of the local drivers are generally very courteous and obliging.

PRACTICAL TIPS FROM A TO Z

Accommodation

Most accommodation is geared towards package tours; individual travelers who haven't booked in advance won't find it easy to find suitable and inexpensive accommodation in the tourist centers during peak season. Tourist information offices in the islands provide lists with prices and descriptions.

The Spanish authorities have divided hotels, boarding houses and apartments into categories, but these only apply to furnishings. So the number of stars or key symbols an establishment may have says nothing about the actual quality of the service and the atmosphere there.

The official categories for hotels range from luxury (5-star) to simple (1-star); for apartments from high-class (3-star) to simple (1-star) and for boarding houses from pleasant family-run establishments (2-star) to very simple places (1-star) with shared bathrooms and lavatories. The categories in the *INFO* section on pages 50-53 have attempted to take atmosphere and service into account as well. The prices are based on the following scale:

⊙ Simple: Double rooms up to 5,000 pesetas.

⊙⊙ Medium: Double rooms from 5,000 to 10,000 pesetas.

⊙⊙⊙ Luxury: Double rooms over 10,000 pesetas.

If you're interested in vacationing in a **Finca** (a country farmhouse, often recently renovated), your local travel agency at home or one of the offices on the islands can provide you with further details. The EU project *Turismo Rural*, whereby old buildings are being renovated and turned into holiday homes, offers good places.

Camping is not very widespread on Gran Canaria. Some beaches have become unofficial campsites, but this is just a tolerated exception to the rule. Communal or private campsites outside the nature reserves are rare, and not usually very peaceful. Camping without a permit is naturally forbidden inside the nature reserves, and even at the official locations you still have to get a permit in advance from the environmental or national park authorities (tourist offices provide more information on this). It's worth making the extra effort to get the permit, however, because of the beauty of the sites. Never camp in narrow ravines (*barrancos*) however – they're prone to falling rocks and boulders!

Banks

Banks are open Monday through Friday from 9 a.m. to 2 p.m., Saturdays to 1 p.m., and slightly longer in summer and during carnival season. If you're exchanging cash or traveler's checks (maximum 25,000 pesetas per check), remember that rates and commissions vary from bank to bank. Exchange outlets and hotels (unfavorable rates!) will change money and checks outside banking hours. Credit cards are accepted almost everywhere, automatic cash dispensers are also a common sight (see "Currency Exchange," pp. 85-86). If you lose checks or credit cards, block them instantly.

Crime

The Canary Islands are generally regarded as relatively safe. Violent crime is rare, but petty crime does exist, especially on the large islands with all the tourism, urban poverty and drug problems. If you leave your car parked in a remote location, make sure you take all valuables out – and also leave the glove compartment open so that it's clear the car has nothing inside. Deposit your valuables in the hotel safe, especially in vacation villages. Also beware of free trips to buy cheap goods. If you agree to one of these, make sure you can assess the quality of what you're offered and check whether it might not be cheaper at home. The best-case scenario here is usually the loss of one day's vacation. If you get taken to a time-sharing location, don't sign anything resembling a contract. Proper firms allow people plenty of time to consider the whole thing, and provide consultations with experts and legal advisers.

On some very busy promenades you may get tricked out of your cash by professional tricksters (e.g., shell games) working together with seemingly uninvolved bystanders.

Customs Regulations

As long as the Canary Islands are not fully integrated into the EU, the customs regulations for entrance into the EU are the same for those of a non-EU state: the duty-free allowances are 200 cigarettes (or 100 cigarillos or 50 cigars or 250 grams of tobacco), one liter of spirits, and two liters of wine.

Once the islands have been fully integrated into the EU, and assuming no special regulations apply, the duty-free limit for import into an EU country will be 800 cigarettes (or 400 cigarillos or 200 cigars) and 90 liters of wine (or 10 liters of spirits or 20 liters of liqueur).

Disabled Assistance

The *Fundación OID* (*Organización Impulsora de Discapacitados*) provides help and information for the disabled. Their Gran Canaria office is located in Las Palmas at Calle Manuel González Martín 22, tel. 928-292315.

Electricity

The tourist centers have the two round pin sockets familiar from France and Germany, so bring an adapter. Current is 220 volts. Some places still have 110 to 125

volts AC with sockets that need an extra adapter, too.

Emergencies

The emergency number to call on Gran Canaria is 092. For first aid or a medic, call 061. The number for the fire department is 080.

Gratuities

In bars and restaurants service is generally included in the bill, but good service is rewarded with a gratuity of around 10 percent of the price. In hotels, chambermaids and porters are given a suitable amount on arrival and departure, especially if they clearly go out of their way to assist. Cab drivers expect around 10 percent of the fare. Outside the tourist centers, people are more ready to help without shooting calculating glances at your wallet.

Medical Treatment / Pharmacies

Medical treatment on the island is good almost everywhere. The hospitals are of European standards. Hotel receptions, tour operators or the consulate will give you the location of the nearest emergency station or medical practice. Many towns and even some small villages have first aid stations operated by the Red Cross (*Cruz Roja*).

Pharmacies (*farmacias*; normally with a green or red Maltese cross on the sign), are open Monday through Friday from 9 a.m. to 1 p.m. and 4 to 8 p.m., and Sat from 9 a.m. to 1 p.m. Pharmacies in every large town have night and emergency opening hours (*Farmacia de Guardia*). The signs outside them tell you which one is currently open.

Thanks to good hygiene conditions, visitors hardly ever get sick. The most common ailments are caused by the change in climate and in diet. Give your body some time to adapt – avoid overdoing things on day one, eat food that's easily digestible, and drink a lot of liq-

Guidelines

uids, but not too much alcohol (if at all). Avoid long periods of sunbathing without proper protection. The tap water is perfectly okay, and you can brush your teeth with it without worry (see also "Health," pp. 84-85).

Opening Times

There are no firmly fixed opening times for businesses. Most stores are open Monday through Friday from 9 a.m. to 1 p.m. and 4:30 to 7:30 p.m., and Saturdays from 9 a.m. to 2 p.m. In the vacation resorts these times are more flexible depending on the season and the amount of business, and some stores are even open on Sundays.

Photography

A large selection of film material is available in the tourist centers, but it's rather more expensive than in other parts of Europe or the U.S. Check the "sell-by" date. Film is also developed overnight in the tourist centers, and the prices are moderate.

Post Offices (Correo)

Generally speaking, all the windows are open in post offices from Monday through Saturday (9 a.m. to 1 p.m., also the one for general delivery). In the big towns the main post offices are also open in the afternoons, and some don't even break for lunch.

Stamps for normal letters and postcards cost 65 pesetas for EU countries, 75 pesetas for non-EU European countries, and 95 pesetas for overseas destinations. Stamps can also be purchased at tobacconists, souvenir stores and hotels.

Public Holidays

The following are official public holidays in the Canary Islands:
January 1: New Year's Day (*Año Nuevo*).
January 6: Epiphany (*Los Reyes*).
March 19: St. Joseph's Day (*San José*).

May 1: Labor Day (*Día del Trabajo*).
May 30: Canaries Day (*Día de Canarias*).
July 25: St. Jacob's Day (*Santiago*).
August 15: Assumption Day (*Asunción*).
October 12: Day of the Spanish-Speaking World (*Día de la Hispanidad*).
November 1: All Saints' Day (*Todos los Santos*).
December 6: Constitution Day (*Día de la Constitución*).
December 8: Immaculate Conception (*Immaculada Concepción*).
December 25: Christmas (*Navidad*).
Moveable Feasts: Maundy Thursday, Good Friday, Easter, Whitsun, Ascension Day and Corpus Christi. Easter Monday, Whit Monday and Boxing Day are not public holidays in Spain.

The tourist offices on the individual islands provide more detailed information on religious festivals, pilgrimages and carnivals.

Swimming / Nude Sunbathing

Swimming in lonely bays without surveillance can be very dangerous because of the powerful undertow and often sharp rocks. The surf can be tricky, especially on the windward side of the island. On beaches where there is surveillance, signal flags tell you whether swimming is currently forbidden (red flag), only recommended for experienced swimmers (yellow flag) or allowed for everyone (green flag). Especially clean beaches fly blue EU flags.

You'll need to wear beach sandals in the black sand here, because it gets very hot – and footwear is also useful as protection against stones when you enter the water. Sun protection is also absolutely essential!

In most tourist centers, topless bathing has become a regular feature on the beach and by the pool. Nude sunbathing is severely frowned upon, however, and is only tolerated at the central section of the dunes of Maspalomas.

Telecommunications

You can dial abroad directly from phone booths bearing the words *internacional* or *interurbana*, either with coins or with phone cards. The latter, known as *tarjetas telefónicas*, are sold in 1,000 and 2,000 peseta versions from post offices, kiosks and souvenir stores. In the tourist centers you can also make phone calls from public phone offices (*teléfonos publicos*) without using coins. The number of units simply gets added up at the end of the call.

The code for dialing abroad from Spain is 07. After you hear a beep, dial the country code followed by the area code minus the initial zero, then the phone number itself.

No code is needed for calls within the island. The previous code, 928, has become a fixed part of the number now.

National directory assistance can be reached at 003, and international information at 025. From Europe to the Canaries you dial 0034 for Spain and then the number.

Time

The time on Gran Canaria is the same as that in the U.K., i.e., Greenwich Mean Time, or one hour behind Central European Time, and changes over at summertime as well – so there is no need for English visitors to adjust their watches.

PHRASEBOOK

The official language on the Canary Islands is Spanish. In tourist centers you'll find that most people understand English pretty well, but a basic knowledge of Spanish is useful if you travel inland.

All words ending with a vowel, an "s" or an "n" and without any accent, always have their penultimate syllable stressed. All other words are either stressed on the syllable with the accent or – if there isn't an accent – on the last syllable. For instance, *Los Cristianos* = los cristiAnos;

El Escobonal = el escobonAl; *Andén Verde* = andEn vErde. Syllables with non-accented diphthongs count as one syllable, e.g., *Antigua* = antIgua; but: *Garafía* = garafIa.

Good morning	*Buenos días*
Good afternoon	*Buenas tardes*
Good evening (early evening)	*Buenas tardes*
Good night	*Buenas noches*
Hello! (between friends)	*¡Hola!*
Goodbye	*Hasta la vista*
Bye	*Adiós*
See you later	*Hasta luego*
See you tomorrow	*Hasta mañana*
How are you?	*¿Qué tal?*
Thanks a lot	*Muchas gracias*
Not at all	*De nada*
Please	*Por favor*
Go ahead	*Sirvase Usted*
Excuse me	*Perdón*
Yes	*Sí*
No	*No*
Do you speak English?	*¿Habla Usted inglés?*
I don't understand Spanish	*No entiendo español*
Speak more slowly please	*Un poco mas despacio, por favor*
What's your name?	*¿Cómo se llama Usted?*
My name is ...	*Me llamo ...*
I live in	*Vivo en ...*
(Very) good	*(Muy) bien*
Help!	*¡Socorro!*
Turn left	*A la izquierda*
Turn right	*A la derecha*
Keep straight on	*Siempre derecho*
How far is that?	*¿A qué distancia está?*
What time is it?	*¿Qué hora es?*
Up	*Arriba*
Down	*Abajo*
Here	*Aquí*
There	*Allí*
Who?	*¿Quién?*
Where?	*¿Dónde?*
Where to?	*¿Adonde?*
When?	*¿Cuándo?*

Guidelines

91

How much?. . . . . ¿Cuánto?
Where can I get ...? . . ¿Dónde hay ...?
What does that cost?. . . ¿Cuánto vale
    esto? ¿Cuanto cuesta?
The menu please!. . . . . . ¡La lista de
    platos! ¡El menú, por favor!
The bill please! . ¡La cuenta, por favor!
Do you have a room free? . . . . ¿Tiene
    Usted una habitación libre?
Double Room. . . . . Habitación doble
Single Room. . . Habitación individual
For one night . . . . . . Para una noche
For one week . . . . . Para una semana
Can I see the room? . . . ¿Puedo ver la
    habitación?
I want to rent a car. . . . . . . Quisiera
    alquilar un coche
I want to rent a boat . . . . . Quisiera
    alquilar una barca
Yesterday. . . . . Ayer
Today . . . . Hoy
Tomorrow . . . . Mañana
Last night . . . . Anoche
Day after tomorrow . . Pasado mañana
Day before yesterday . . . . . Anteayer
Holiday . . . . Día festivo

Days of the Week

Monday. . . . . Lunes
Tuesday . . . . Martes
Wednesday . . . . Miércoles
Thursday . . . . Jueves
Friday . . . . Viernes
Saturday. . . . . Sábado
Sunday . . . . Domingo

Months

January . . . . Enero
February . . . . Febrero
March . . . . Marzo
April . . . . Abril
May . . . . Mayo
June . . . . Junio
July . . . . Julio
August . . . . Agosto
September . . . . Setiembre
October. . . . . Octubre
November . . . . Noviembre
December . . . . Diciembre

In a Restaurant

Today's menu . . . . . . Menú del día
Dessert . . . . Postre
Bread . . . . Pan
Drink . . . . Bebida
Wine . . . . Vino
Beer . . . . Cerveza
Mineral water. . . . . . Agua mineral
Carbonated/uncarbonated . Con/sin gas
Black coffee. . . . . Café solo
Coffee with a little milk. . Café cortado
Milk coffee . . . . . Café con leche
Breakfast . . . . Desayuno
Lunch . . . . Almuerzo
Supper . . . . Cena
Omelette . . . . Tortilla
Potato omelette. . . . Tortilla Española
Soup . . . . Sopa
Meat . . . . Carne
Beef . . . . Carne de Vaca
Pork. . . . . Cerdo
Veal . . . . Ternera
Chicken . . . . Pollo
Lamb . . . . Cordero
Fried . . . . Frito
Grilled . . . . A la plancha
Baked. . . . . Asado
Salad . . . . Ensalada
Vegetables . . . . Verdura
Peas and beans . . . . . . Legumbres
Fish. . . . . Pescado
Sea pike . . . . Merluza
Trout. . . . . Trucha
Salmon . . . . Salmón
Tuna . . . . Atún
Swordfish . . . . Pez espada
Squid . . . . Calamares
Octopus. . . . . Pulpo

Numbers

0 . . . . cero
1 . . . . un(o), una
2 . . . . dos
3 . . . . tres
4 . . . . cuatro
5 . . . . cinco
6 . . . . seis
7 . . . . siete
8 . . . . ocho

AUTHORS

Bernd F. Gruschwitz is a historian and Anglicist, and lives in Bremen. He has been a regular visitor to the Canary Islands since 1986, as a photographer and travel guide author. He wrote the chapters "Gran Canaria – Holiday Island to Suit Every Taste," "Canarian Cuisine," "Arts and Crafts on the Canary Islands" and "Flora and Fauna." For Nelles Verlag he has additionally worked as an author and photographer on *Nelles Guide Bali/Lombok* and *Nelles Guide Prague*.

Michael Reimer is a photographer and the author of a number of travel, hiking and cycling guides, as well as numerous articles published in trade journals. He wrote the "Historical Overview," as well as the features "Adventure Hiking" and "Demanding Cycle Tours."

Wolfgang Taschner is a specialized freelance journalist as well as a travel guide author. He generally concentrates his writings on the field of active nature holidays. He has written numerous books on the Canary Islands, which are among his favorite travel destinations. For this book he contributed his expertise and experience in the features "Dreaming of Marlin," "Magnificent Diving," "Greens beneath the Palms" and "Surfboards in the Breeze."

PHOTOGRAPHERS

Guidelines

INDEX

Explore the World

NELLES MAPS

AVAILABLE TITELS

Afghanistan 1 : 1 500 000
Argentina *(Northern)*, **Uruguay**
  1 : 2 500 000
Argentina *(Southern)*, **Uruguay**
  1 : 2 500 000
Australia 1 : 4 000 000
Bangkok - *and Greater Bangkok*
  1 : 75 000 / 1 : 15 000
Burma → *Myanmar*
Caribbean - **Bermuda, Bahamas,**
  Greater Antilles 1 : 2 500 000
Caribbean - **Lesser Antilles**
  1 : 2 500 000
Central America 1 : 1 750 000
Central Asia 1 : 1 750 000
China - *Northeastern*
  1 : 1 500 000
China - *Northern* 1 : 1 500 000
China - *Central* 1 : 1 500 000
China - *Southern* 1 : 1 500 000
Colombia - **Ecuador** 1 : 2 500 000
Crete - Kreta 1 : 200 000
Dominican Republic - Haiti
  1 : 600 000
Egypt 1 : 2 500 000 / 1 : 750 000
Hawaiian Islands
  1 : 330 000 / 1 : 125 000
Hawaiian Islands – **Kaua'i**
  1 : 150 000 / 1 : 35 000

Hawaiian Islands – **Honolulu**
  - **O'ahu** 1 : 35 000 / 1 : 150 000
Hawaiian Islands – **Maui - Moloka'i**
  - **Lāna'i** 1 : 150 000 / 1 : 35 000
Hawaiian Islands – **Hawai'i, The Big**
  Island 1 : 330 000 / 1 : 125 000
Himalaya 1 : 1 500 000
Hong Kong 1 : 22 500
Indian Subcontinent 1 : 4 000 000
India - *Northern* 1 : 1 500 000
India - *Western* 1 : 1 500 000
India - *Eastern* 1 : 1 500 000
India - *Southern* 1 : 1 500 000
India - *Northeastern* - **Bangladesh**
  1 : 1 500 000
Indonesia 1 : 4 000 000
Indonesia **Sumatra** 1 : 1 500 000
Indonesia **Java - Nusa Tenggara**
  1 : 1 500 000
Indonesia **Bali - Lombok**
  1 : 180 000
Indonesia **Kalimantan**
  1 : 1 500 000
Indonesia **Java - Bali** 1 : 650 000
Indonesia **Sulawesi** 1 : 1 500 000
Indonesia **Irian Jaya - Maluku**
  1 : 1 500 000
Jakarta 1 : 22 500
Japan 1 : 1 500 000
Kenya 1 : 1 100 000
Korea 1 : 1 500 000

Malaysia 1 : 1 500 000
West Malaysia 1 : 650 000
Manila 1 : 17 500
Mexico 1 : 2 500 000
Myanmar (Burma) 1 : 1 500 000
Nepal 1 : 500 000 / 1 : 1 500 000
Nepal Trekking **Khumbu Himal -**
  Solu Khumbu 1 : 75 000
New Zealand 1 : 1 250 000
Pakistan 1 : 1 500 000
Peru - Ecuador 1 : 2 500 000
Philippines 1 : 1 500 000
Singapore 1 : 22 500
Southeast Asia 1 : 4 000 000
South Pacific Islands 1 : 13 000 000
Sri Lanka 1 : 450 000
Taiwan 1 : 400 000
Tanzania - *Rwanda, Burundi*
  1 : 1 500 000
Thailand 1 : 1 500 000
Uganda 1 : 700 000
Venezuela - Guyana, Suriname,
  French Guiana 1 : 2 500 000
Vietnam, Laos, Cambodia
  1 : 1 500 000

FORTHCOMING

Bolivia, Paraguay 1 : 2 500 000
Chile 1 : 2 500 000
Cuba 1 : 775 000

Nelles Maps are top quality cartography!
Relief mapping, kilometer charts and tourist attractions.
Always up-to-date!

GRAN CANARIA

ISBN 3-88618-775-6

90000>

9 783886 187751

Destinations: Gran Canaria, which gave the Spanish archipelago its name, is a continent in miniature. The many facets of this island make the busy city of Las Palmas in the north, the impressive volcanic landscapes of the island's center, and the golden sand dunes of the south all equally interesting to sun worshipers and active vacationers alike.

Travel Information: The *INFO* section at the end of the travel chapter recommends hotels, restaurants, museums and events. The features on fishing, diving, windsurfing, golf and cycling also provide you with addresses of major operators on the island. The *Guidelines* chapter will help you prepare for and get the most out of your holiday.